1

IN YOUR BLOOD:
Football culture
in the late '80s and early '90s

British Library Cataloguing in Publication Data

Turner, Richard 1965-
   In your blood: football culture in the late '80s and early '90s.
   1. Great Britain. Association football. Social aspects,
   history.
   I. Title
   306.483
   ISBN 1-870736-07-9
   © Richard Turner 1990

Cover design by Cliff Harper
Typesetting by Cecilia and Ed

CONTENTS

INTRODUCTION

If there was ever an example of a particular issue becoming a case of paranoia and hysteria for the public, press and politicians, then surely the football supporter is it. In a nation notorious for stereotyping groups of people, the way in which every person who happens to enjoy attending football matches has been tarred with the image of lager swilling, nationalist thugs has been among the most deeply ingrained on the minds of the establishment - and the least challenged.

The staggering passion of football fans for the national game has bemused those who do not have soccer in their blood. Football is not 'just a game' as are other sports, it is a whole way of life. Bill Shankley summed up the feeling when he said that football was more important than life and death. The stereotyping and fear of football fans as some sort of sub-human grouplet on the fringes of society is largely due to a failure of British society to understand the game and its followers.

It must be stated that the 'average football fan' would be immensely difficult to pinpoint. Although it is a largely working class male spectator sport, football draws its devotees from all walks of life.

Supporters have been categorised into those who stand on the terraces and those who sit in the stands, who are seen as older and wealthier fans who have often previously stood on the terraces in their younger days. Attempts at categorisation such as this are usually sunk by the numerous exceptions - for example, many people watch matches from the terraces all their lives, whereas some groups of young and vocal fans are to be seen in the seats of many grounds.

Almost every football ground in the country has an 'end' where the home supporters tend to congregate to urge their team on and to give a show of strength to away fans. The ends are the most important part of the grounds for many fans, it is their territory, a place to meet friends and to have a good laugh. The Taylor Report could mean the phasing out of terracing and an end to the focal point of football culture for thousands of people.

Wherever you happen to sit in most grounds or whoever you are, there is often no way to escape biting wind, queues for lousy food and a host of other appalling facilities. If a person supports a team which consistently loses every match and play in a pre-war wind tunnel, it must be difficult for an 'outsider' to comprehend the mentality of the fans.

Yet the feeling of camaraderie on the terraces and the feeling of invincibilty stood packed into an end with others as devoted as you is unique to football. The exhultation of seeing your team win makes all the hardship worthwhile. Football matches are a social event for most fans, a chance to meet friends and get away from all the world's troubles - but the prospect of winning is still the major driving force behind the support.

It goes without saying that football is not a faultless form of entertainment. The point is that the media and politicians have made a huge issue of the hooligan element and reaped the political rewards of its condemnation, but it took the disasters at Bradford and Hillsborough to raise the issue of the safety of football fans.

The fans have almost no say in the running of the sport that they pay to keep going. The powers that be have taken no notice partly because of the media image of fans, an image which they too have accepted unquestioningly, and because money and power are more important than any concept of customer satisfaction.

Soccer hooliganisn was not new to the n..d and late 1980s, rather it was an ongoing feature of life on the terraces until it reached a climax with world headlines after rioting Liverpool fans caused Juventus supporters to crush against a wall that collapsed at the European Cup final at Heysel in 1985. 39 people died and the spotlight of public attention was turned on the football supporter in general. Since Heysel, violence on English football terraces has lessened, largely due to developments in policing and a change in the fans' attitude to terrace fighting from a harmless show of male aggression to a serious threat to the game itself. Obviously, violence associated with football is not near to ending, but has become more organised outside the grounds and the international arena seems to be the new battle ground. Other countries now have their own hooligans blatantly modelled on the English examples they have seen when England have played there.

Those supporters who indulge in violence are not representative of football fans and are a small minority of crowds. However, I do not agree that hooligans are not interested in the game, as the football authorities allege - the violent element are often among the most devoted and this may be what contributes to their desire to fight for their club. The hooligans are present at most games, whether it be a match with potential for confrontation or a low key match where there are very few away supporters.

Some clubs are slowly starting to realise that their ordinary supporters are important and that they cannot just expect them to keep turning up and paying ever increasing entrance fees, getting little in return. This increased awareness has coincided with soccer fans becoming more organised to give their views a coherent voice. This was most obviously evident after the Hillsborough disaster with Rogan Taylor of the Football Supporters Association finally giving the 'general public' some home truths on the conditions of grounds for football supporters and the appalling incompetence of those running soccer who take the money but no responsibility for those who are, after all, their clientele.

The first signs of an appearance at grounds of children and women, and the developments of family enclosures, are encouraging signs , but the blatant racism and sexism hardly contributes to a welcoming atmosphere.

And just as things were starting to improve a little, Colin Moynihan appeared on the scene like a bad smell with his compulsory I.D. cards and Football Spectators bill. Fortunately, the Taylor Report put a stop to that in its present form. Politicians of all shades have shown absolutely no interest in football, unless there are votes to be won in condemning hooliganism or turning up at the Cup Final for a press photo-call.

It is argueable that thousands of people massed on concrete steps, chanting in unison and showing unrelenting loyalty to their town or city is anachronistic in these days of mass media and internationalism. But once football is in your blood, you are hooked against all rationality.

The terraces have also provided a showground for many of the youth cults from the '50s onwards, a fashion parade for mainly young males. The closest ties between these trends and football has been in the 1980s, with the soccer 'casual' image that developed into the Acid House phenomenon. Popular cultural images are an integral part of football culture, from the clothes to the chants

8

derived from popular songs. In a society increasingly materialistic, apathetic and unimaginative, the soccer terraces provide a refuge, a chance to be someone and to let off steam.

The Taylor Report could seal the fate of standing on the terraces, particularly for 1st and 2nd division clubs, which would be a tragedy for the game and its followers - it would see the end of the game as we know it, traditions which are well worth defending, despite the game's associated problems.

This work is a general overview of the world of the soccer fan. Specific examples are predominantly from my own experiences in following Fourth Division Stockport County, but many of the points are applicable throughout English league football.

EDGELEY PARK, STOCKPORT.

PART 1

LIFE ON THE TERRACES

For many people, football is not merely a spectator sport but a whole way of life. No other sport instills the same amount of passion in its fans as soccer, and it is these supporters who make the game such a unique phenomena. Football is not limited to 90 minutes per week - it dominates many pubs, homes, schoolyards and workplaces. A whole culture has developed over the last century for those watching professional, and even non-professional, football, a distinct culture that has baffled those who are not under the hypnotic influence. The size of the crowds, the fortunes of the clubs and the styles of the fans have altered with the times, but the central theme of following your team to victory, the game itself and the grounds in which it is played have remained largely unchanged.

The importance of football for mainly working class people lies in the opportunity it provides for getting away from the rigours of everyday life, a chance to yell and shout without a boss, parent, spouse or teacher watching your every move (although recent years have seen the police managing to limit the escapist potential). Any pent up frustration can be discharged in the anonymity of a large crowd, without anyone particularly noticing. Arguments with loved ones, hassles at work and general despair can be thrown aside as you submerge yourself in a game.

Of course, many men and women play football themselves for clubs at varying levels. For some, playing and watching are part of a general love of the game - they enjoy playing on the local park with their mates, but also derive immense pleasure from going to watch the local team play on a Saturday afternoon. Others like to play, but feel bored watching a game, so do not become spectators. Most football spectators enjoy at least a kick around, if only to emulate their heroes on the pitch.

Those who spectate at football matches have been stereotyped by the media, authorities and the public into the image of the football fan as loud-mouthed, aggressive, uncultured and bigoted.

11

This is an unrealistic portrayal simply because soccer fans are drawn from all walks of life, they have different expectations from the game, they are of all ages and are only united by their love of football. The concept of an average fan is ridiculous, even if it could be identified in theory. However, there are elements which make up a general football culture, but no fan adheres to all the elements because some are mutually exclusive.

The match is the highlight of the week for a lot of people. As soon as the workplace or schoolyard discussions over the previous match die down, attention is then turned to the next game. For people who work all week, the weekend is the justification for carrying on - down to the pub on the Friday night and to the match on the Saturday. At Stockport, it is possible to combine both as most of the home games are played on a Friday night because one of the big Manchester clubs plays at home on a Saturday. Tranmere also play home games on a Friday night to avoid clashing with either Liverpool or Everton.

The rivalry in homes, schools and workplaces between fans of different local clubs helps to fuel the passion and contributes to the excitement. At school, most of my friends were Manchester City fans, with a few Manchester United and a smattering of other oddities who supported teams such as Leeds or Liverpool because they were successful. I still hold people who just pick a team to support, and do not even go to watch them, in contempt. Even though I lived in Stockport, there were only a few County fans at school. I used to know most of the County fans who lived in our area, mainly through recognising them at matches or because they were in different classes at the same school. We tended to stick together mainly to counter the ridicule we were subjected to, but also because we had something in common and were proud to be County fans.

At least we supported our local team. The easy option was to follow Manchester City, Manchester United or Liverpool, But it took guts to follow a team that usually lost more games than they won, even at home. Both mates and relatives lampooned our devotion to Stockport County, but I suspect that they had a quiet respect and admiration for us. My grandfather used to tease me terribly after defeats and I used to go on and on to him if we won, but I think he was glad I was a County fan.

Knowing other fans helps maintain the importance a football club plays in communities and fuels the excitement as plans are made for the weekend game, especially away games. I have never thought that following Stockport, even during years barren of success, was strange, but I dare say that it seems irrational to some people.

Football matches are a chance to meet friends for a good evening out. Some people meet up for a drink in the pubs outside grounds in the hour or so before kick-off. Many grounds used to have bars actually inside the gates until hooliganism led to inquiries which blamed alcohol for much of the violence and the bars have largely disappeared now. The pubs are an important part of the lifestyle for many fans. The majority of these go for a social pre-match drink, but, since the introduction of tighter policing in the grounds, the hooligan element also congregate in the pubs, which are usually on the main road between the ground and the railway station.

With the introduction of all-day opening hours, the pubs have become meeting places after the game too, either as the start of an evening out on the beer or as a stop-off on the way home. Of course, it must be stated that the majority of fans just go straight to matches, but pubs play an important role in football spectating for a significant number of supporters.

As with many clubs, Edgeley Park, Stockport County's ground, is situated in a residential area, with narrow side streets surrounding the ground and a shopping centre, unfortunately, a stone's throw away. This is handy if you are a football fan and happen to live near a ground, but once every week or two local people must wish that they lived elsewhere. The fact that many grounds were built in residential areas, rather than out of town, has contributed to the popularity of the game over the last century because it has meant that ordinary people have not had to travel far to watch a game. Fathers are prepared to take sons if there is not far to go, and hence breed a new generation of fans. Kids can get a bus at an early age with their mates to the local ground. Going to matches with a friend was one of the first occasions that my parents let me off the leash, it was an important part of my development as a child. Wearing a County scarf and with my duffle coat firmly buttoned, I felt independent and grown up walking to the ground with other fans.

I was taken to football games at an early age by my dad and uncle, not to every game and I thought of it as a real treat, even though I did not fully understand what was going on. Most people are introduced to the football way of life at an early age, either by parents or mates taking them along. Of course, not every child dragged along to a match latches on to it. I still see a few small children looking bored. On my brother's handful of trips to Edgeley Park he was more interested with how the floodlights worked than who had just scored a 30 yard net buster. A person either takes to football or loathes it, regardless of sex. Many girls love football, but this is repressed by parents who feel that they should be doing something more in keeping with girl's pastimes. Once a person has football in their blood, it is hard to shake off - televised football is a very poor substitute to being present at a game. It was hooliganism that created the armchair fan more than any notion of comfort, which has been the great tragedy of football.

****

Inside the grounds, fans gather in groups of friends until the ground fills up as kick-off approaches. Football grounds are a great place to meet people and a lot of people who otherwise would be lonely or shy can find friendship in grounds by just chatting to the person next to them about team selection, the previous game or, that great British standby, the weather. Part of the appeal of football is that, theoretically, anyone can go to a match - there is no dress code, age barrier or need to go with other people. Of course, black people and women have been alienated from playing a role in football culture by prevailing and deep, ingrained racist and sexist attitudes.

Many grounds have four distinct areas for the fans: the away end, the stands, the end or area where the vocal support gathers and the rest of the terracing. It is difficult to say that a particular type of fan watches the game from a particular area. For example, it is often said that the younger fans all gather in the end and the older fans sit in the seats, but there are exceptions to most of these stereotypical allocations, such as groups of hooligans sitting in the stands and older fans wanting to continue to stand with the younger fans for the excitement.

I like to get into the ground 10 minutes before kick-off so that I can get a decent place to stand, have a read of the programme and because I do not like queueing - although there is not usually much call for queueing at Stockport! At a small club, like Stockport, the same people are often stood in a particular place on the terraces week in and week out. I occasionally wonder if they are conscious that they stand in the same place and what they would do if someone took their spot on a particular barrier. Other fans rarely see a kick-off, either because they are sat in the pub or just do not see the need in getting there early.

Most of the groups huddled on the terraces before kick-off are of a similar age, either middle aged work mates or gangs of kids too young to join their heroes in the pub. Litter starts to amass as soon as the first fans enter the ground. I cannot ever remember seeing a litter bin in a football ground, apart from a few bigger grounds with a dustbin near to the refreshment kiosk. No-one ever seems to mind the rubbish, probably because they are only there for a couple of hours and presumably litter bins are perceived as potential weapons - perhaps the idiotic phenomenon of missile throwing is a fan's litter removal system!

At kick-off, most people are in the ground. There is no other feeling like standing in a crowded part of the ground, it is a strange blend of being an anonymous face in the crowd, but everyone being considered a friend. This camaraderie, a feeling of invincibility, is a key element in football culture. Life on the terraces is generally good-humoured, apart from the increasingly rare outbreaks of hooliganism. The language of football fans is coarse, to say the least, but this is the result of high excitement and the fact that many fans are ordinary people who see no need for verbal restraint. I do not consider swearing to be a problem, the same choice expressions can be heard in homes, workplaces and schoolyards. Much of the shouting involves biting humour, with a particular person yelling a philosophical insult at the referee, linesman or anyone who is listening.

In his report into Hillsborough, Lord Justice Taylor talked of the "stench of stewed onions" in grounds, this is mixed with an odour of sweat and cigarette or pipe smoke. With a fall in the number of smokers, football crowds are still hovered over by a pall of smoke - perhaps this is just the stress of watching Stockport County! Some young people start to smoke at football matches because they are under pressure to act hard and are influenced by older fans who smoke. The smell of football grounds is quite distinctive if you specifically try to identify it, but is not particularly noticeable after a while.

Most of the grounds in England are very old, even dating back to the turn of the century. Until very recently little consideration has been given to the safety of soccer fans. The ironic thing is that it is the fans who contribute the most money to the game, but are treated as turnstile fodder by the clubs. Disasters, such as those at Ibrox in 1971 and Burnden Park in 1946, and a number of inquiries failed to influence anyone in authority that the fans are actually individual, ordinary people.

It took years of hooliganism and alternative mass media entertainment, leading to falling attendances, before anyone in authority realised that something was drastically wrong. A combination of falling profits and the development of a grass roots consciousness among the fans have slowly started a re-appraisal of the whole game by the media and the football authorities. Further disasters at Bradford, in which 55 died in a fire in the main stand, with its subsequent Popplewell Report, and Hillsborough have finally forced changes in the comfort and safety of football supporters.

Most clubs would not be prepared to admit that their supporters have been given a raw deal in the past, but they do pay more attention to the wishes of their fans in the 1990s than previously. However, the profit motive is still important and the spate of property developers interested in grounds is an alarning phenomenon. The rumours of ground sales have abounded for years and this has helped fuel the fans' unity. Stockport County have repeatedly been reported as moving to a new ground, but the only English club who have actually moved to a new ground by the end of the 1989/90 season are Scunthorpe.

The issue of the actual ground is difficult for fans as many would like to have a brand new stadium if they had a say in the design, but there is a perhaps deeper loyalty to grounds which are haunted by good and bad memories. I would hate to see a move from Edgeley Park, if only because it is a part of my life and the history of the town I come from. Stockport County are aware of the rumours but have stated that, for the time being, they are aiming to improve the facilities of the Edgeley Park site.

I, like thousands of other people, derive immense pleasure from standing on the concrete terracing. Most of the smaller clubs' grounds are basic in their layout, usually with a covered terrace, an open terrace and a main stand. Covering is frequently sheets of corrugated iron, there is grass growing on the terraces of some grounds and many grounds convey a general atmosphere of shabbiness. Fortunately, there is a growing awareness of the aged nature of grounds and that, if the conditions are improved, then attendances could well improve.

Stockport County realised this and have concreted the terracing at the Railway End, which is where the away fans now stand. This end used to be soil and shale, with rotting railway sleepers for terracing which used to get slippy when wet. Pens and fences have been erected for away fans, but there is still no shelter for away fans who choose to stand - the club acknowledges this, but finance for such a major task is difficult for small clubs. On the "Popular" side along the length of the pitch,the club have put a back onto the covered stand to reduce the considerable draught and wind which blew rain and snow under the covering.

The two biggest complaints of fans about conditions have been about toilet facilities and refreshments. I vividly remember being astounded at the sight of a man urinating into a rolled up newspaper at a match when I was younger - apparently, this is common at bigger grounds. The problem is that toilets are too few and are difficult to reach in a dense crowd. Toilets in football grounds tend to be no more than open sewers which are dark, smell appalling and have inadequate space. Recently, Stockport and a few other clubs have built new toilet block with lighting, a metal raised trough urinal and a generally cleaner condition. There is one toilet for women, which is more than some clubs, but this covers the whole ground and the club states that more are desirable.

Food and drink for football fans has always been a standing joke. Tea has been cunningly disguised as coloured hot water served in plastic cups that have an uncanny knack of spilling their contents without warning. Pies, described as meat and potato have provided fans with hours of endless fun in 'hunt the meat'. A selection of over-priced confectionary and pre-packed cold drinks have made up the 'menu'. The range and standard of food varies dramatically from club to club. I used to enjoy going to away games to check out the pies and compare grounds on their merits. Some grounds stick in your memory , such as Wigan who used to serve chips from a van and had Heinz soup! Food is particularly important for away fans who may have travelled hundreds of miles. This fact is starting to be appreciated by clubs. If the fans have been escorted to the ground from the train station, their only opportunity for food will probably be in the ground. Many clubs have improved the standard of their food provision with better pies, burgers and even baked potatoes, but the speed of this improvement again varies from club to club.

An article in the Caterer & Hotelkeeper, on 17th August 1989, highlighted the improvements in catering with an analysis of Electrolux starting to run kiosks at Luton, Coventry and West Bromwich Albion. Electrolux has invested £100,000 in Coventry for a restaurant, they intend to keep their kiosks open until the match is over and not just half-time, and they intend to train their staff to serve quicker.

A big problem is the number of refreshment kiosks in the grounds. As in the toilets, long queues develop and it is difficult to get out of the crowd to obtain a pie. Spending half-time queueing for a cup of Bovril may be a traditional part of watching a football match, but this could be eased with a bit of planning and more outlets which are strategically placed. Some clubs have people bringing food round the pitch, which helps to ease the demands on the kiosks, but more improvements are needed.

****

Gate money is the largest single source of revenue for football clubs. The cost of admission to football matches is rarely grumbled at. To stand on the terraces at Stockport County costs £3-50 in the 1989/90 season and £4-00 in the 1990/91 season, which are fairly typical prices. There are reductions at most grounds for junior supporters, the defined age of which varies from club to club, and the amount of 'under 16 year olds' with moustaches and the smell of beer on their breath is amusing. £4-00 is quite a large chunk out of a giro or low income, but is only an outlay once a fortnight and this is the one 'luxury' a lot of people choose to spend their money on. The cost of watching a football match is more than a night out at the cinema, but cheaper than the majority of professional, live entertainment, such as concerts.

The problem is that many non-sporting spectator entertainments have a guarantee that certain standards of production will be maintained, if the actors in a play repeatedly forget their lines, the audience will ask for their money back. This sort of customer guarantee of satisfaction simply does not apply in the same way, and does not seem to be expected from the fans. It takes a disasterous series of results and behind-the-scenes buffoonery on a surrealist scale to get the fans demonstrating, and this is rare. Even in these times of more awareness of the views of the fans, even the most militant supporters only want better conditions to watch the match and a say in the running of the club - the fact that there may be a totally crap game, with football worthy of a Boy Scout's team and the ball boys dropping off to sleep, fails to stir up more than a chant of "What a load of rubbish" and a section of the crowd wandering off to the pub 15 minutes early. Obviously, there are a few loud mouthed critics who bemoan the conceded goal in a 6-1 win, but they sum up the diverse nature of the supporters rather than indicate mass disillusionment with a particular performance. Generally, there is an attitude of taking the rough with the smooth and the resilience of the fans' patience is more noteworthy than the falling attendances.

****

It is not the conditions themselves that have contributed to fans staying away from football, as there have been similar conditions for years. However, people's expectations and demands from entertainment are higher so that, even if not responsible for falling attendances, the facilities in football grounds need to be improved to welcome new fans and persuade them that there is a little bit of civilisation in the game. More significant to keeping people away was the aggressive atmosphere that developed in the 1970s. However, with a few notable exceptions, outbreaks of hooliganism inside the grounds are now unusual and clubs are starting to woo back the fans.

Stockport incorporated the concept of 'The Friendly Club' into their public image, which has become more positive in recent years. 'The Guardian', on 14th April 1990, reported on a woman who wrote to Tottenham for mementoes for her children but received no reply, she then wrote to Stockport, where her family had used to live, and received a bundle of scarves and stickers.

Several clubs are involved in community projects aided by financial help from the Football Trust. These include provision of creches, social clubs for the elderly and the encouragement of women's football. This extension of the clubs' activities into the community is excellent, but has a long way to go and, again, varies from club to club.

Stockport, as with many other clubs, have allocated part of the ground as a family enclosure, which comprises several rows of seats where parents can sit in comfort and safety with their children. If the family enclosure idea works in introducing young supporters to the grounds, then it is obviously worthwhile and commendable.

****

Although polls have shown that the fans want better facilities in the 1990s, the main concern is still the game itself. The chance to see your team win is what makes most people go down to the match. The sense of euphoria after a goal is scored is beyond compare and there is an electric buzz eminating from crowds if their team is winning. The great feeling of winning and the way in which the world looks rosier makes all the bad times worthwhile. A win puts you in a much better mood and, no doubt, the friends and families of fans pray their team wins so that there is no sulking. The driving force behind the support of football is the hope that, one day, your team might get promoted - although most of the time it takes an irrational loyalty to sustain the dream.

Loyalty to a team is essential, even if this can be severely tested if you follow a team languishing in the depths of the lower divisions. Football provides an opportunity to give vocal support to your town. I often end up hoarse after yelling at the players to urge them on, but feel that my support can help the team's performance. When the team is playing badly, some supporters barrack them, usually picking on a particular player to blame - or the manager. As fans are paying customers, perhaps they are entitled to criticise a poor performance, but this has to be tempered by loyalty and support. The moods of fans are notoriously volatile because expectations vary from fan to fan, and from club to club. In the 1989/90 season, a successful campaign for Stockport County, with expectations raised sky high after years of mediocrity, the critics were quickly out for blood after a series of poor results. Fortunately, a strong run at the end of the season brought the smiling faces back and Stockport reached the play-offs. However, if the players are obviously not trying hard, then they are letting the fans down in the same way as those who criticise when the players are losing, but doing their best, are letting the team down.

****

The reduction of hooliganism inside the grounds during the late 1980s was partly due to stricter policing and surveillance of fans. However, the policy of tighter policing has led to all fans being treated as animals, which has only served to fuel the trouble and deepened the resentment felt by many fans. Even in the 1990s, the treatment of fans by the police leaves a lot to be desired because there is little effort made to distinguish between ordinary fans and hooligans. Away fans in particular are herded into one part of the ground, kept under constant observation and are liable to be ejected from the ground on the whim of the officers. It has been alleged, and with a significant degree of truth from the fans' point of view, that police forces use the match on a Saturday to let their officers off the leash.

Fans are intimidated by police horses and dogs while they are queueing to get into the ground and walking to and from the match. There is little consistency in policing from one area to another and behaviour that would pass unnoticed in most places can get you arrested at a particular ground. A police officer may laugh and joke with you, but his or her colleagues will be hostile and aggressive. It seems that the police often provoke trouble or eject fans either to keep arrest numbers up or out of boredom. New police equipment and tactics are often tried out on football fans before entering general use, an example of this is the 'Hoolivan' with a camera on top which is now in general use.

Many fans have stories of being assaulted by the police or seeing people being arrested for doing nothing wrong. It is possible that the police treat fans this way because of the image that is portrayed of football fans as all being potential yobs or because of their previous experience with the violent element. But there is no excuse for treating one set of people any differently than the rest of society and their behaviour reinforces the stereotype. There is a great deal of mistrust between police and fans, which is a hindrance in the development of grounds with a friendly and relaxed atmosphere.

Football brings out deep emotions in people and, as long as it is just verbal outbursts, then there should be no need for the police to interfere. Insensitive policing can lead to bitterness. An example of this was on the last home game of the 1988/1989 season when Stockport fans were prevented from holding a traditional end of season celebration on the pitch. There is very little communication or liaison between the police and supporters' clubs and the police are rarely helpful in giving information to away fans, seeming to begrudge any civility. The ultimate aim must be to have grounds where no police are needed and the stewards are able to organise the crowd - sadly, this is rather utopian at the moment. The clubs would also like to see the role of the police reduced, if only because the police bills are so high. The average police bill at Stockport for the club is c.£1,000 and the club has little say in how the match is policed.

****

As football has developed since the 1950s, the concept of the youth cult has emerged also and this has frequently been reflected in the fashions on the terraces. Most fans have, of course, continued to wear the accepted norms in dress sense, but skinheads, punks and the flared trousered youths of the '70s have all put in an appearance on the terraces. Most of these youth cults have had their roots in music and their appearance on the terraces is coincidental rather than a driving force behind the mode.

The 1980s, however, saw a working class football style have its base on the terraces, rather than in music. This became known as the 'soccer casual'. As the soccer firms developed, the competition was not only in fighting, but also style. The soccer casual look was a practical dress code with trainers as footwear, rather than 'bovver boots', bleached or stone-washed jeans and expensive sweaters and T-shirts. Pringle and Tuccini were initially the in-wear, but this rapidly changed as groups and individuals sought to outdo each other. Wealthy fans, of particularly London clubs, added expensive jewellery to their outfits.

Many fans did not wear their colours, the firms certainly didn't, and it was often difficult to tell fans of different clubs apart. The only identification to ascertain who was on who's side were small enamel badges declaring loyalty to a particular team. The soccer casual was only representative of a small proportion of the crowd, but they developed a distinctive football-based lifestyle.

The soccer casual developed throughout the 1980s. The emergence of the Acid House scene in the late 1980s added new colour and zest to many of the ends. The hairstyles which had been the 'perry' cut, with a long fringe and short back and sides, were replaced, in some cases, by longer hair for the 'second summer of love'. A particularly alarming feature was the re-appearance of flared jeans and cords by the Manc scallies. However, the soccer casual of 1989 and 1990 was more likely to have a shaved back and sides, be clean shaven, with jeans, T-shirts and trainers still in vogue. many fans took to wearing replicas of their club or country's shirt. Tattoos are an important way for many young fans to express their permanent loyalty to team and country. Ear-rings are also an acceptable accessory, but these are often not worn, or replaced with sleepers, for big games where the risk of having them ripped out is higher.

The catwalk for this gear is the pubs and terraces where fashion is used to show off to other fans, is part of the display of hardness and to attract members of the opposite sex. It is important to re-emphasise that there are no particular features of football culture that apply to all fans and the soccer casual image was only adopted by generally younger fans.

One particularly bizarre trait was that of the inflatables in the 1988/1989 season - what happened to them all is anyone's guess. Among the first fans to bring them along were Manchester City's with huge inflatable bananas. The inflatables serve no purpose, they are cumbersome and are merely waved about, yet they proliferated in that season. Many fans had their own produced to reflect their team's image, such as Grimsby's haddocks and Norwich's canaries. The general inflatables appeared at all grounds, these included bananas, cigarettes, sharks etc. Stockport, rather oddly, adopted turtles as their speciality because several fans worked for one of County's sponsors, Turtle Wax. The inflatables made the grounds friendly and provided everyone with a laugh, only Arsenal disapproved and sought to ban them from Highbury. As quickly as they appeared on the scene, they disappeared, and in the 1989/1990 season were a rare sight. A little bit of soccer history disappeared along with the football rattle and kids standing on orange boxes to see better.

For some people, attending home matches does not provide them with their fix of football, especially as there may be only one home game in 2 or 3 weeks. Travelling to away games has been made easier with improved road and rail links, and supporters organising coaches and trains. Watching your team away is great fun. Travelling to a town or city that you would otherwise never see in your life, such as Peterborough or Lincoln, is all part of the experience. Many fans travel with a few friends in a car, but I think that the best way to see an away game is to go with a lot of other fans. The people who go to away games are usually diehards who you recognise anyway.

Away games may mean travelling hundreds of miles on weekday evenings. For example, in the one season that I attended every home and away match (I was at school then, which was great in the holidays, but meant that I had to get several jobs to pay for it all) Stockport played at Colchester on a Friday evening, which involved getting back to Stockport at 4am on the following morning.

Going to away games when the team is not doing well and losing most of their games can be a bit of a disappointment, but this is made up for if the players come over to thank you for going at the end of the game. There are usually a couple of players at least who relate to the fans, Mickey Quinn (now doing very well at Newcastle) was one notable example.

It is a wonderful feeling stood with a large following of Stockport fans. On the last game of the 1989/1990 season, Stockport took 4,000 fans to Halifax. It was brilliant to see hundreds of small children in County kits shouting the team on and exuberent fans spilling onto the pitch when Stockport scored. To win away is one of the best parts of being a football fan. If your team scores at home, the fans clap and cheer, but if you score away everyone goes absolutely beserk!

The problems of travelling away are the cost incurred, in train fares, food, drink and entry to the ground. Also, away fans have been liable to attacks from home supporters, although this seems to be declining. The police seem to be hostile to people from out of town and treat all away fans as if they have no right to be there. If your team has lost badly, the return trip can be monotonous. In the ground, you often have no say where you can watch the game from, which sometimes means getting soaked through if there is no cover in rain. But these are minor qualms and, generally, away games are a great laugh and an important part of the football way of life for many fans.

PART 2

CHANTS

Football fans do not sing, they chant. Any comparison with skills involving a modicum of musical talent would be absurd. Even the players are incapable of singing, despite the variety of club records which have only served to highlight this. Most fans and players would be happy to admit that they are happier at a match than in a recording studio (with the possible exception of Kevin Keegan!).

Chanting is part of the uniqueness of soccer, it is almost the only sport where spectators urge their team on by united vocal support - although games such as rugby are starting to adopt soccer-style chanting and cricket occasionally receives the dubious honour of an appearance by 'footie fans' attracted by the hot weather, a lack of football between May and August, the novelty of a game where players are allowed to pick the ball up and a bar open all day. The very word 'chant' conjures up religious associations and, for the devoted football fan, perhaps this is apt.

The vocal support is used to urge on whichever team you support by yelling the name of the club, such as "We love you Stockport, we do. We love you Stockport, we do. We love you Stockport, we do. Oh, Stockport, we love you!" or just the name alone, the tune for this usually depends on how many syllables there are in the name. Most chants are pretty basic, involving the repetition of one or two lines, so that everyone knows the words and a semblance of synchronicity can be maintained. The basic core of chants are adapted by almost all clubs.

Apart from urging on the players, chanting is also used to cast aspersions on the referee's parentage when decisions go against your team. A current favourite is "Where's your father, where's your father, where's your father referee? Haven't got one, never had one, you're a bastard referee!" to the tune of Waltzing Matilda. Others include "You black bastard etc." and "Who's the bastard in the black?" (presumably no-one has a programme). Any hair loss or physical deformity on the part of the referee or linesman is the signal for merciless abuse. In general, however, it is all pretty lighthearted and you get a grin out of the official (but they are still bastards!).

Soccer fans are merciless in their targets of ridicule, everything from the police taunted with "Harry Roberts is my friend" and the Laurel and Hardy theme tune to the women who are dragged out for presentations on the pitch at half time being treated to choruses of "Get your tits out for the lads". The mentality of football (clubs included) in its treatment of women has an awful long way to go before grounds are realistically welcoming to all.

"Sack the board" is another popular song at the end of the season at many clubs. Peter Swales at Manchester City receives more than his fair share of this. Players and managers do often get an honourable mention from the terrace choirs, but fortune is a fickle thing and a lack of success will turn praise into hate. In the same way, there is a thin line between "We'll support you ever more" and "What a load of rubbish" in defeat, usually depending on the mood of the leading chanter and the standard of the team's performance.

Many of the more 'sophisticated' songs (relatively speaking, of course)are derived from pop songs or traditional folk songs. This reflects the importance of working class culture on the game. The words may be re-arranged, which is where the art lies. "You'll never walk alone" by Gerry and the Pacemakers was left almost unchanged to become the anthem for Liverpool's Kop. West Ham adopted "I'm forever blowing bubbles" and so on. Newcastle United's anthem is the "Bladen Races", developed from a 19th century popular song and still boisterously sung by the Mags' fans, but no-one else (presumably because no-one else can understand a word they are saying!)

Most supporters use the chants to pass on stories of great victories in the past both on and off the pitch. It may seem slightly absurd to class this as a form of oral history, but that is what it is in practice. An example of this is the following chant, which has been passed on through several generations of Edgeley Park's faithful:

"At the turn of the century, in the clear blue skies over Edgeley,
Came a roaring and a thunder like you've never heard
When Stockport County had scored their third.
Out on the pitch, the boys in blue,
We beat Palace and West Ham too.
Their fans tried and their fans died
And were buried together on the Popular Side.

27

10, 20, 30, 40, 50 or more
The West Ham fans could take no more.
We used our heads and we used our feet
And they run like fuck down Castle Street!"
There are plenty of other examples of this glorying in past incidents of violence. Of course, these are mindless chants to outsiders, but they are part of the folklore for football fans and doubtless other clubs have songs about kicking the living daykights out of Stockport's fans.

Most of the chanting occurs where there are large numbers of away supporters. The aim is to make more noise than the opposing fans, so that the players are aware of the superiority of your vocal support. F.A.Cup matches and local derbies have the best atmosphere because there are two sets of fans making as big a racket as possible. Players have frequently stated that they respond to the atmosphere in grounds.

The opposing fans bare the brunt of much of the chanting. This varies from having the score chanted at them if they are losing to the ever reliable "Sing when you're winning" if the score favours the opposition. The size of the away following is always good for a laugh. The handful of diehards who have travelled hundreds of miles on a cold Friday night might be treated to the crooning of "Come in a taxi, you must have come in a taxi". This has variations such as "Come on a tractor, you must have come on a tractor" for any club who have even the remotest connection with rural existance; "Come on a skateboard" for very small away followings or "Come in a condom, you couldn't come in a condom" for when the game is getting dull. The ultimate ignominy is for the away following to chant "You're supposed to be at home" or "What's it like to see a crowd" at the home fans.

Barracking of away fans ranges from sheep noises directed at the supporters of Welsh and Yorkshire clubs to the delightful refrains of "You're gonna get your fuckin' heads kicked in!" Most of this is an expression of loyalty to your town or city. The sick culmination of this is the Scouse taunting of Manchester United fans with "Munich '58" and the Manchester reply of "Shankly '81". This may well be the tasteless extreme, but there is a genuine fierce loyalty for home towns, particularly smaller clubs who live in the shadow of bigger clubs. An example of this is Tranmere, who are based in Birkenhead over the Mersey from Liverpool and Everton. Their fans have the classic "Don't be mistaken, don't be misled, We're

28

not scousers, we come from Birkenhead!". Stockport, apart from a seemingly universal hatred of Manchester United, have the surreal "Oh Stockport town is wonderful, Oh Stockport town is wonderful, Full of what? Full of shops, shops and more shops, Oh Stockport town is wonderful!"

Ex-players re-appearing for the opposing team are usually greeted with "Stockport reject", although the player usually rejected Stockport. Even less easily forgiven are managers who left under a cloud - and when they left, they were followed by half the team to their new club, then things can get really vindictive. A case in point, and no doubt every club has at least one, is Colin Murphy, the legendary linguist famous for his unintelligible programme notes. Murphy left Stockport for Lincoln City and several of Stockport's players followed him there. The Stockport 'boys' devised the following charming epitaph to Murphy's memory:

"There's a tavern in the town, and we're gonna burn it down,
We're gonna hang Colin Murphy from the highest tree
For all the Lincoln fans to see!"

Football fans do not seem to mind being considered weird by the rest of society, the game is all that matters to most. Philosophy in defeat is essential, especially if your team is consistently losing. The media image of football supporters is of hooligans and social misfits. There is little that the supporters can do to counter this stereotyping against the might of the media and public opinion, although a few clubs' fans play up to it all tongue in cheek. In the 1970s, Manchester United's fans tried to live up to their, then very poor, reputation with chants of "We hate humans!" Millwall, whose name is dragged through the mud more than most, philosophically reflected that "No-one likes us and we don't care", which became the title of a T.V. documentary on Millwall's fans. Chelsea and England fans have come up with the alarming "Let's go fucking mental!", which seemed to alarm the Italian police no end during the World Cup.

Then there are the downright ludicrous, such as Chelsea's "One man went to mow" or the group of Stockport fans, complete with foam wheelbarrows on their heads, singing "I've got a wheelbarrow, the front wheel is bent" ad nauseum.

Of course, soccer fans are a mixed bunch of people, to say that they are all cloth capped, Labour voting men is utterly out of date in the 1990s. Among those gathered in the ends, a minority, albeit vocal, still have National Front leanings if only through peer pressure - if they knew what the other policies of the fascist groups were, apart from the racism, they would probably ridicule that too. Occasionally, Ulster loyalist songs are heard on the terraces, such as "UDA, all the way. Fuck the Pope and the IRA" or "Give me hope in my heart I pray, give me bullets for my gun, so I can shoot them one by one, those bastards from the IRA"

However, during the miner's strike of 1984/5 after the Mansfield miners had returned to work, at a Stockport versus Mansfield game, there was an almost constant chant of "Scabs, scabs, scabs!" from all parts of the ground, aimed at the away fans. More recently, at several games in 1990 there were a few chants of "We won't pay the Poll Tax", which no doubt had the government shaking in their boots! This latter case is one of the few exceptions to the rule of political activists taking their chants from the terraces, notably "Here we go, here we go, here we go!"

Chanting at football matches is pretty harmless. I would rather have fans yelling at each other than kicking the living daylights out of their rivals, terrifying other fans. The chanting usually only comes from one part of the ground and if people don't like it then they can stand elsewhere. It can act as a safety valve for pent-up frustrations of everyday life. I used to go along to 'sing' my heart out and hurl abuse - we still usually lost, but I felt a hell of a lot better after. I would not argue with the Taylor Report's recommendation that racist chanting ought to be outlawed as it raises tensions and makes grounds unfriendly places. However, the proposed ban on swearing smacks of authoritarianism and the inevitable conclusion of this would be to ban chanting completely (there are a few cases of this happening already, with the police arresting people just for chanting the club's name). No chanting would mean that a part of the traditional atmosphere of the terraces would be lost. Of course, the language is coarse, soccer fans are ordinary people who, when excited, are bound to come out with a few choice expletives. Would a ban on swearing mean that the police and players would have to stop? And would the ban be extended to language in workplaces and pubs? - highly unlikely.

"We never win at home
and we never win away.
Stockport County
O.K.?!"

30

FOOTBALL AND THE
EXTREME RIGHT

Racist chanting occurs at most, if not all, soccer grounds in the League. Black players are barracked by ape noises from sections of the crowd, usually this is only directed at players of the opposing team. The majority of supporters accept black players on their own team because they are 'one of our boys'. Stockport County used to have a very popular black player, Oshor Williams, who was accepted and even the racist element on the Popular Side would chant "Oshor is white" to justify their support for a black player - he became, in effect, an honorary white to some fans.

I would argue that British society is a racist society and, although racist chanting at football grounds is particularly blatant and aggressive, the racism present in many fans is a reflection of racist attitudes inherent in the world outside soccer grounds. This is in no way meant to condone racist chanting. The chanting and abuse goes almost totally unchallenged so that many, particularly young, supporters see nothing wrong in using terms such as 'nigger', 'Paki', 'coon' etc. and this leads to contempt for the rights of blacks, Asians and Chinese outside football and the terrifying levels of racially motivated attacks in our communities.

Also, football grounds are generally still white enclaves, even in areas where there are communities of ethnic people. A few teams, such as Arsenal, do have black fans, but they are few and far between. It must be horrific to be a black fan watching a football match among hundreds of frenzied white youths chanting things like "Zigger, zigger, zigger, Shoot that nigger" etc. It is hardly surprising that very few black fans are prepared to put up with that.

The irony of it all is that the black players are often among the most talented on the team. It has been alleged that this is because of racism in the clubs themselves, in that only the very talented black players manage to get on the books of League clubs. Another irony is that many of those chanting racial abuse have black friends at school, work or in the pub.

There are a few supporters who never accept black players as part of their team and would much rather have white players in their place. I have met a number of such-minded fans, notably a

31

group of Chelsea supporters who declared that if a black Chelsea player scored they did not count that goal! This sort of conflict between team and race is a poor reflection on these fans and their allegiance to their team.

Racism, at whatever level in society, is never seriously challenged by governments because it divides the masses and keeps them from questioning more important issues than the colour of a person's skins. This simmering racism is picked on by extreme right-wing political groups, such as the National Front and the British National Party, to recruit members. The role of neo-fascist groups within football culture varies from club to club, but it is important to appreciate that it still does exist.

The National Front reached the peak of its' popularity in the mid 1970s with a membership of c.17,000. The election of Mrs. Thatcher in 1979 stole much of the thunder from the N.F. and the Front lost much of its' support to the Conservatives. Splits within the N.F. have further weakened the party and in 1990 the faction that produced the National Front News disbanded itself.

However, if the internal politics of the Front proved to be chaotic in the 1980s, the populist nationalistic policies proved to be attractive to some of the disillusioned young working class, faced with unemployment, dead end jobs or training schemes. A combination of immigration as a scapegoat for unemployment and a jingoistic government (culminating in a war over the Falkland Islands) created a climate that was rife for the N.F. to exploit.

Racism at football matches and the political ideas of the National Front are two separate entities, but the N.F. has achieved a degree of success in harnessing them. The link was made by the Young National Front who produced a magazine called 'Bulldog', which was aimed at young football fans and was edited by Joe Pearce (who served two jail sentences for distributing racist literature). 'Bulldog' aimed to channel the frustration of fans into a racialist political ideology, mainly by a direct racist statement of 'Wogs out'. In addition, 'Bulldog' printed league tables of football hooligans to encourage links between the Y.N.F. and hooligans.

The skinhead variety of fascist is a rare sight at football games. I have seen skinheads ridiculed, abused and physically assaulted by soccer casuals because of their appearance. It must be pointed out that the skinhead youth cult is not inherently racist or fascist, most are not involved in the N.F. and many skins are active anti-fascists.

Not all clubs have active National Front groups within their supporters. Fascist paper sales are limited to particular clubs and some of these are carried out by units who sell the papers and do not even attend the match. I have never seen a paper sale outside Edgeley Park, but there are N.F. sympathisers and literature is occasionally read by pockets of fans on the terrace.

It is easy to over-exaggerate the numbers of N.F. members in soccer crowds, but their significance lies in the influence a few can exert, notably in starting racist chanting which other fans join in with.Rather than fully paid up members, it would be more accurate to say that some fans sympathise with the racialism and hatred of the IRA that the N.F. propose.

The National Front's annual Remembrance Day parades are often supported by soccer casuals, such as the Chelsea Headhunters or Leeds' Service Crew. The British National Party rallies in racially tense areas are largely made up of soccer fans (the B.N.P. having little skinhead backing). Both the N.F. and B.N.P. have linked up with soccer firms to attack Irish Republican marches in Britain.

A number of clubs have a consistent and high profile fascist presence, the most notorious being Chelsea and Leeds, but also including clubs such as Blackburn, Portsmouth, Newcastle and Aston Villa. The blatant racists are a minority in all crowds and other fans have, in a few places, felt sufficiently offended to organise against the nazi element. This is usually carried out with the help of the local trade unions and anti-fascist groups - examples of these campaigns are 'Leeds United Against Racism and Fascism' and Newcastle's 'Geordies are black and white'. Such campaigns have an important role to play and are particularly brave considering that the vocal racists are usually the hardest. I think that I would have serious reservations about going up to a group of sieg-heiling fans to tell them that I didn't agree with what they were doing because I have to stand alongside them in future matches and I value my physical welfare. I believe that there are thousands of people afraid to speak out because of a fear of getting a kicking for their trouble.

Obviously, the black players are aware of the abuse and banana skins. Luther Blisset declared, in a Daily Mirror report on 10th April 1987, "Normally the abuse is from the terraces, but at one Leeds game whole groups in the stand were doing nazi salutes and shouting 'Sieg Heil'". Andy Gray, in, of all papers, 'The Sun', said, "Elland Road is the worst ground of the lot ... I couldn't handle the abuse, black bastard and things like that." Generally, though, the racism stirs up black players to play better to shut the barrackers up.

The role of the N.F. in actively organising soccer violence is hard to define. There is certainly evidence of hooligans contacting each other to arrange fights, but whether they are N.F. is unclear.

However, there is more concrete evidence of far right groups organising 'crews' for England matches. This partly explains the phenomenon of fans, who are usually kicking each other all over the place, linking up to fight (although the main reason is pure nationalistic fervour). Anti-fascist groups have gathered evidence of N.F. supporters contacting European nationalist football followers and of N.F. banners and literature at England matches where violence has occured.

Anti-fascist groups allege that the rioting at Heysel, which led to the disaster, was instigated by N.F. supporters. There are also reports that N.F. and B.N.P. leaflets were found on the terraces and that some of the Liverpool banners had fascist symbols on them e.g. 'Liverpool Edge Hill' with a swastika. Allegations also abound that Italian fascists were among the Juventus fans who continued rioting after the wall had collapsed. How true all this is is open to debate, but it is certain that a significant number of football fans are sympathetic to the extreme right-wing groups.

The fact that groups such as the National Front have been able to exploit the frustrations of young, working class males at football grounds is an indictment of the failure of the police to recognise the problem of racism, of the clubs for turning a blind eye to the issue and of the Left for failing to address the frustrations and offer realistic alternatives to the scapegoating of particular sections of society for problems created by the government.

Because ordinary fans are afraid to stand up to racist thuggery, because of a very real fear of ridicule, abuse and physical violence, all fans continue to be labelled with the image created by the minority.

FASCIST PAPER-SELLERS OUTSIDE ELLAND ROAD, LEEDS.

THE RACIST LEAGUE

CHELSEA have been knocked off the top of the Racist League! Chelsea supporters have been the most racist in the land for years but now they have a real battle on if they want to get back to the top.

But it's not their arch-rivals, Leeds United, who have deposed them from the top spot. No, the new leaders in the Racist League are Newcastle United whose loyal supporters are becoming notorious for their pro-British and pro-White views.

Leeds United stay in second place while Chelsea drop to third position. But Blues fans are still the most racist in London, staying ahead of West Ham in fourth position and Millwall in ninth.

Rangers fans are easily the most patriotic supporters in Scotland. They are the only Scottish team in the top ten. While Coleraine keep the edge on Linfield as the most patriotic in Northern Ireland.

Second Division Portsmouth are promoted into the top ten of the Racist League, while First Division Norwich are relegated.

RACIST LEAGUE — TOP 10

1. NEWCASTLE UNITED

2. LEEDS UNITED

3. CHELSEA

4. WEST HAM

5. GLASGOW RANGERS

6. COLERAINE

7. PORTSMOUTH

8. LINFIELD

9. MILLWALL

10. BIRMINGHAM CITY

FASCIST PROPAGANDA (ABOVE) AND OPPOSITION TO IT (BELOW).

HOOLIGANISM

There had been violence at football matches for at least 20 years before the 1985 Heysel disaster. The media are particularly fond of digging out newspaper clippings, from as early as the turn of the century, charting reports of unruly behaviour by football fans. It is possible to trace working class violence associated with ball games even further, to the 17th century and the traditional mass football games on Shrove Tuesday. However, it was the 1970s that saw the appearance of the 'boot boys' on the terraces.

Soccer hooliganism developed out of the away club's supporters turning up in significant numbers at grounds to support their team. Improvements in rail and road communications made it easier to travel to other towns and cities. The away fans are a separate body of fans because of their vocal support for the opposing team, their colours, their accents, if the two teams are from different parts of the country, and, more recently, they are kept segregated in a separate part of the ground. A large number of supporters who travel to watch their team away are young and boisterous. Away games are a great excuse for a day out for young people, a chance to get away from the town where they may spend their whole life and to see their team play other than just home games once a fortnight.

Segregation of home and away fans developed in the 1970s as a response to the rising incidence of hooliganism. Segregation inevitably leads to a 'them and us' feeling. The concept of ends, or the part of the ground where most of the home fans stand, plays an integral part in the terrace fighting. The home fans consider their end to be their domain and are prepared to fight to defend it. The away fans aim to take the end by steaming into the home fans, creating panic and mayhem.

During the 1980s, Stockport fans aimed to take various grounds. These were usually clubs near to Stockport because large numbers of away fans are needed to take an end and because there is added prestige in taking the end of a club in the same area as yours. News of away fans taking an end has an uncanny knack of being spread among other clubs' fans, even without the aid of the media.

Every club develops a particular rivalry with another club, this

37

is usually the closest. For Stockport fans, the favourite ground was probably that of Crewe Alexandra at Gresty Road. Many Stockport fans were disappointed when Crewe were promoted to Division 3 and there were to be no more trips out to Crewe.

As stated previously, by the 1980s, soccer violence had reached such a scale that away fans had realised that it was not a good idea to wear scarves, as they were liable to get a good kicking for their trouble. For teams who are geographically close to each other, this led to confusion about who was on who's side, if the accents were similar. Because of this, Stockport fans were able to infiltrate the home fans' end at Gresty Road.

It is a nerve wracking experience entering the home fans' territory and looking for people you recognise. Occasionally, the home fans would notice you immediately and a hasty retreat was called for. The basic idea is to enter the ground in small, inconspicuous groups and gather some way from where the home fans are massed. The away fans slowly walk towards the home 'boys'. The away fans will usually chant the club's name, such as 'Stockport boys, we are here!', as loud as possible to get the adrenalin going and to give the impression of greater numbers than there may actually be. Immediately after this, there would be a charge into the home fans to try to create panic so that all the home fans would run. There is an immense feeling of power and pride as an end opens up in front of the away fans.

The home 'boys' usually organise themselves to fight back, but such terrace punch-ups are usually over in a couple of minutes. A few blows are exchanged, but generally much of it is macho posturing, with both sets of fans urging the other to 'come and have a go', but wariness often getting the better of bravado. The police usually pile in quickly to force the away fans onto the pitch and round to the away supporters' enclosure, where they are greeted by the rest of the away fans like returning conquering heroes. A few might be ejected from the ground, even fewer would be arrested. This was the scenario of much of the fighting inside the grounds during the early 1980s.

This sort of behaviour is what sociologists probably label machismo, fans proving their manliness to themselves and others. Perhaps this may be so, but the main thing I have noticed is the appeal of the excitement, fear and nerves associated with hooliganism which gets the adrenalin going in the same way as sex does. In a 'Guardian' article, on 6th April 1990, a Leeds fan was reported as saying, "Experts say it started because of bad housing, unemployment ... That's a load of rubbish ... Fightings entertainment". Most of the lads I knew at Stockport came off the estates that proliferate in the town, they were on the dole, training schemes or in low paid jobs. Those who were involved in fighting did it because it was exciting, the highlight of the week. A few of the older fans were employed in white collar jobs or well paid manual jobs. The notion of well paid professionals being involved just for kicks never really applied at Stockport, although I am reliably informed that other, particularly London, clubs' fighters have included teachers, accountants etc.

The 1st round of the F.A.Cup is always a big occasion and, if there is an away draw, an early start. Telford and Runcorn have been recent non-League hosts to Stockport's fans, who have arrived early with no police. Running battles took place, windows of houses in Runcorn were smashed and the 'Buck's Head' pub in Telford was wrecked in scenes reminiscent of a wild west saloon bar. It must be emphasised that Stockport's fans are by no means the worst, even in the lower divisions.

The towns I have always felt sorry for are those which are seaside resorts and have a League football team. They attract the largest away following with people turning up for short holidays, lots of beer and a punch-up with the town's football fans. At the end of the 1989/90 season, Bournemouth were treated to a visit by Leeds fans, who promptly rioted after incompetent scheduling and ticket details led to thousands being locked out. When Scarborough were promoted to the Fourth Division, they must have wondered whether it was worth it after their first game erupted into several days of violence involving Wolves' fans. The televised scenes of fighting, destruction and the unforgettable picture of one fan falling through the roof of one of the terraces highlighted the problem for seaside resorts.

Blackpool was a great day out for hundreds of Stockport fans. The 'Dutton Arms' pub, on the sea front, bore the brunt of the drunken violence. Early in the 1989/90 season, I saw the 'Dutton Arms' on television, again all smashed up, this time by Birmingham City fans.

Strangely, it is Torquay that has been mainly on the receiving end of Stockport's seaside adventures. Stockport is about 400 miles from Torquay, but they seem to have the misfortune to play Stockport at home in the holiday season. A friendly weekend away usually ends up in fights with the local constabulary as Torquay either have no fans prepared to fight or they are not around when needed. Games against seaside teams frequently attract away fans who would not normally travel and even people who do not support the team at all, but go away for the weekend with their mates who do.

The early 1980s saw a great deal of terrace fighting, pitch invasions en masse and general mayhem. However, there were rarely any major injuries in the grounds and it was all treated as a huge joke - a chance to prove who had the hardest fans. But the proportion of any crowd who are prepared to fight is very small and these punch-ups often terrified the life out of the majority of other fans, who just wanted to watch the football in peace. As the trouble continued in the grounds, many fans gave up standing on the terraces and even football matches altogether because they were not even able to take their kids along, without the risk of being crushed or caught up in the violence. Being involved in terrace gangs was not particularly dangerous, but it was ruining the game for everyone else and creating an atmosphere of hatred.

The mid 1980s saw hooliganism taking a more ominous turn, with the appearance of close-knit groups of fighters, who developed a lifestyle around the violence and began to organise themselves into exclusive elites. These fans were mainly young, in the 16-30 age group, and fashionably dressed - they became known as 'soccer casuals'. There had been hooligans in the 1970s and earlier, of course, but not as dedicated as these and on such a well organised scale. The fans involved in these crews needed money to travel, buy clothes and drink - to live the life of the cool, professional soccer hooligan.

Loyalty to whatever the town or city the fan comes from is an essential part of the hooligan mentality. Hatred of other areas takes on nationalistic proportions.

Drinking was still an important part of the lifestyle. Dutch courage was acceptable, but to get very drunk meant that that fan was a liability in any fighting. Basically, the pub was a place to meet outside the grounds, in the same way as the end was the meeting place inside. Most, if not all, League teams had their crews of fighters. The bigger teams, with the hardest and most notorious fans, even had names for their crews of hooligans. The most famous are the Chelsea Headhunters, West Ham's Inter City Firm, Leeds' Service Crew, Manchester City's Governors, Birmingham's Zulus etc. Many of these firms used calling cards to leave with their victims.

Ironically, it was an increased awareness of the problem of terrace violence, and it's impact on attendances, that led to the growth of these tightly organised groups. With a Conservative Party in power, based partly on a law and order ticket, outbreaks of sporadic violence could not be tolerated. The straw that broke the camel's back was the televised riot of black and white Millwall fans at Luton, where police were chased across the pitch under a hail of missiles and hundreds of seats were ripped out. The days of hooligans risking ejection from the ground, or a small fine if arrested, at worst, for fighting were almost over.

The fact that it took until the late 1980s for anything to be done at all is remarkable, considering that the incidents of the 1960s and 1970s had been escalating all the time. In 1968, in the Harrington Report "Soccer hooliganism: a preliminary report", it was stated, "... it would be foolish to rule out the possibility of much more serious crowd disturbances at football matches than we have yet experienced" and "We feel that improved ground facilities would not only help to deal with the hooligan problem, but do something towards its prevention. Clubs often seem keener to spend money on the purchase of players than to undertake any major spending on ground improvements which would increase safety and make hooligan control easier". The government has manipulated the spectacle of soccer hooliganism to detract from other issues and to justify its more reactionary law and order legislation.

The 1980s saw policing at football grounds become a military style operation, to the point where it borders on the oppressive and labels all fans as potential yobs. Fences were erected to prevent pitch invasions and the fans getting at each other on the terraces. Segregation of away fans from home fans became the norm and supporters were penned into different parts of the ground. Fines for football related offences became much higher than for similar offences committed in other walks of life.

Perhaps the most effective weapon in the fight against hooliganism was the introduction of the closed circuit television cameras. Again, this had been suggested for years, but was not acted upon. In 1969, the Lang report stated "... the view was formed that closed circuit television could be of value in the general subject of crowd control and ... would be an important factor in preventing misbehaviour by spectators at grounds".

41

The football hooligan merely changed tactics with the changing times.

The home fans had used to gather in their end and wait for any trouble from the away fans, but they now found that the policing was getting too heavy and so transferred their operations outside the grounds. The concept of turning football grounds into fortresses merely penned ordinary, decent supporters in and put up huge fences to obscure their view of the game - and ultimately, the horrific consequences of Hillsborough. Violence in the grounds did fall sharply and arrests in the 1989/90 season were down on the previous year. However, the fighting was now on the streets, at railway stations and in pubs - shifting the innocent victims of violence from ordinary, peaceful fans in the grounds to passers by who have nothing to do with football at all.

With violence outside grounds, weapons could be used in attacks, whereas they would have been found by police searches at the turnstiles. Away supporters arrived early in towns, with no police escort, to go drinking and pick fights with locals, not necessarily soccer fans. Television documentaries have filmed the crews in action in railway stations and outside pubs. Fans have been killed in the fighting outside grounds.

It is an absolute fallacy to say that hooliganism is limited to certain notorious groups of fans attracted to First and Second Division football. The violence involving followers of lower division and even non-League clubs is as vicious and frequent. This is partly because there are less police, less expectation of trouble and the fans all tend to know each other, so stick together if anything happens. My most terrifying moments have come from the supporters of teams like Burnley, Bolton and Port Vale - this may sound funny and perhaps their crews are only relatively large and hard.

The trouble with all this is that, if you are a young male and want to watch your team away, you cannot wear a scarf and are usually on edge until you get into the away fans' enclosure in case you are sussed out by home fans. It then all starts again at the final whistle and the journey home.

Picking off lone fans or stragglers is an easy and popular tactic for home 'boys'. I have only had this happen twice, at Wigan and Tranmere, where I was chased but not caught! Any lad or group of lads is fair game for football fans. To be fair, however, there is an unspoken code that means that women, children and old people

42

do not get attacked. Machismo at least spares a few innocents. If the home fans are unsure whether a set of fans who have just come out of the station are away fans, the aim is to find out their accents, where this would be relevant. Merseyside fans use the old gem of "Got the time on you, mate?" and when the person replies, obviously their accent is revealed.

It must again be pointed out that the notion that hooligans are not real supporters is nonsense and is only used as an attempt to shame them. The same people who enjoy a fight at the big games also turn up on cold, weekday evening games against teams with few fans. They are also among the devoted fans who travel away when there is no potential for trouble. Violence is merely a part of the culture of soccer for certain supporters. Different people do get different things out of watching football,

The large scale reduction of violence inside football grounds would seem to give some credence to the football authorities' claims that the remaining violence outside the grounds is society's problem and not theirs. But this is not strictly true and the passing of the buck between football authorities and the government has given the hooligans years of breathing space. The government has repeatedly said that football must put its own house in order, yet then comes up with a piece of oppressive legislation in the Football Spectator's Act. The football authorities, of course, don't give a damn about the fans and have washed their hands of the violent element, despite the fact that it besmirches the game they purport to represent.

It is the police who have been left to respond to the increasing violence associated with football. The policy of penning all fans in and keeping them under careful surveillance has kept the hooligans at bay. However, the attitude of the police to soccer fans has been zealous, to say the least, and assaults on supporters are common. Again, the image of soccer fans as hooligans has meant that the police have been given a free rein as no-one in authority is going to say that the police are ill-treating fans. Perhaps the actions of some fans could justify police officers losing their tempers, but the contempt with which all fans are treated is unacceptable and unfair. Also, the well-worn cliche that if you treat people like animals, they act like animals, has a certain amount of truth in it.

It is not difficult to join one of the crews and the police have managed to infiltrate a number. The information gathered has led to a series of police raids on suspected yobs. The most famous of these was 'Operation Own Goal' in May 1987 against Chelsea fans, followed in the same year by raids leading to the arrests of 36 Birmingham Zulus. In theory, this is a good way of bringing the violent element to justice without harrassing ordinary, peaceful fans. However, as has been well documented, many of these undercover operations collapsed, either because of doubts over the integrity of the young, and often inexperienced, police involved or because of administrative errors in the prosecutions. However, many fans still consider this tactic as still valid because it does not interfere with the game of football and its supporters.

The development of closer ties between the clubs and their supporters may possibly bring a sense of belonging and responsibility to some fans. 'The Friendly Club' concept is aimed at bringing more people back to the game and alienating the thugs even more within the grounds.

In Lord Justice Taylor's final report into the Hillsborough stadium disaster, Taylor states that a review of all the previous reports into soccer's ills leads to a number of conclusions. These are the effectiveness of closed circuit television, which is generally accepted at last. Voluntary membership cards and segregation are also urged, along with more seating, the encouragement of supporters' clubs and involvement of the club in the community. The other suggestions of a ban on alcohol and heavier penalties are in force to a greater or lesser degree.

However, these recommendations are aimed at tackling the serious image problem afflicting football. It should be obvious by now that there is no catch-all solution to the violence associated with football. To remove the problem from this particular sporting arena to somewhere else is surely no solution at all.

A slightly different case is that of hooliganism by English supporters in Europe. The 1970s and early 1980s saw frequent examples of thousands of supporters following their club into Europe for the various European tournaments, causing mayhem in the towns and cities they visited. Leeds were suspended because of the behaviour of their fans and most of the other big English clubs' fans were involved in incidents abroad. Although the media, government and authorities ranted on about how terrible it all was, nothing was ever done. The destruction continued, which is how hooligans of other countries picked up their tricks of the trade. In

44

the 1980s, the violence intensified, with ferry companies refusing to carry football fans, stabbings becoming commonplace and a Spurs fan being shot dead by a bartender in Amsterdam's red light district. The hypocrisy of the government was staggering, sending 'our boys' to the Falklands on a wave of jingoistic fervour, instilling hatred of foreigners and then being appalled when England fans stormed through Europe fighting all-comers. Driven on by a heady mixture of nationalism and alcohol, disaster was inevitable.

May 29th, 1985, was merely the logical conclusion of a failure of authorities at all levels to realise the scale of the problem of hooliganism by English fans in Europe. The European Cup Final in 1985, between Juventus and Liverpool at the Heysel stadium in Belgium, was supposed to be the showpiece event of the footballing year. It ended in hours of rioting, which led to a wall collapsing under the pressure of Italian and Belgian supporters fleeing from rampaging Liverpool fans. By the end of the night, 39 people were dead.

The major cause of the Heysel disaster was Liverpool fans throwing missiles and charging at Italian and Belgian fans in the next section. The legal proceedings against the handful of Liverpool fans prosecuted are still continuing. However, bearing the main reason for the disaster in mind, it must be pointed out that the incompetence of those running football in Europe is often on a similar level to their English counterparts. Complaints about the standard of the Heysel stadium for major games had been voiced previously. It may well be that better policing, segregation and ticket allocation may have prevented the disaster.

It was inevitable that English clubs would be banned from Europe and it was only in July 1990 that the ban was lifted. This has not meant that European soccer is free from violence. A second wave of hooliganism, inspired by the English example, has involved clubs from almost every European country. This increasingly frequent violence is often more vicious than in England and the authorities in Europe seem to have learnt little from their encounters with the English. A notable example was the riot in Yugoslavia during the 1989/90 season.

Of course, the ban on English clubs was not extended to the national team, so there are still forays into Europe. Many supporters watch England away just for the football, but, again, all are labelled yobs because of the image of England fans as animals, to an even greater extent than the domestic supporters. The

45

England match in Albania showed several hundred fans going to Albania for the World Cup qualifying game, having a great time and making friends with Albanians - of course, there is no news in that, so the media have conveniently forgotten all about it.

England supporters are now expected to cause trouble and there is a sense of disappointment if it all passes off peacefully. Every little incident is translated as a full scale riot by the media, the notable example being the European Nations Cup in Germany in the summer of 1989. Of course, as in England, the behaviour of a proportion of the fans has been aggressive enough to contribute to a justifiably sceptical view of the soccer fan, but if you are a genuine, peaceful soccer fan, this can make life hard. In watching England away, every nutter in that country is out for a fight with the famous English hooligans. Regardless of the fan's willingness to fight, any England fan is fair game. There is truth in the claim that they were often forced to fight just in self-defence. In March 1990, intelligence sources in Italy warned of plans by some Italians to exact revenge for Heysel during the World Cup and, although somewhat exaggerated, gangs of Italians did attack English campsites.

In addition to this, the police and army are usually brought out en masse to deal with the English fans. Many English fans have stories of European police attacking them without provocation. It is the same story as in England, a few idiots have brought about oppressive policing and crowd control for all.

It is difficult to argue that those parts of the Football Spectator's Act relating to restrictions on travel to England matches for convicted hooligans are not justifiable. The only possible flaw in this is that, as in England, occasionally, innocent people are arrested in confusing situations. But, most football fans are sick of being put into the same category as those England fans involved in violence abroad and something must be done.

It may seem melodramatic to say that, while English society (and any others for that matter) is based on nationalistsic sentiments, fighting foreigners is bound to continue, whether at football matches or at holiday resorts, but I believe that this, coupled with the fact that many fans consider it a good laugh, is partly responsible for the hooliganism abroad. 1992 is supposed to bring better understanding and closeness between Europeans, but the easing of travel restrictions is hardly going to have the thugs extending the hand of friendship to each other.

However, closer links between intelligence agencies may pinpoint, isolate and ultimately remove the hooligans from the international football scene. The major drawback to supporting the police intelligence is that the measures that they employ, such as access to more and more data about individuals, will become accepted by many people in cracking down on the movements of soccer hooligans. But then this eases the passage of more oppressive policing on other 'undesirables', such as peace campaigners, anarchists, trade unionists and then anyone who holds any ideas that differ from the accepted norm. The policy of giving the police wide powers to fight hooliganism is an easy option, but the implicit dangers in it for the rest of society are alarming and this will probably just shift the yob element to some other arena.

Again, it seems that everyone is adopting a 'wait and see' approach, with a few half-hearted publicity stunts aimed at restricting the hooligans. The more the media and government rant about hooliganism, the more the hooligans have to live up to, so that violence involving English fans abroad is unlikely to disappear because of some wonderful panacea.

BLOODBATH AS CUP SOCCER FANS RIOT

LIVERPOOL ECHO 5.90

RIVAL armies of battling Yugoslav soccer fans overpowered riot police at a Zagreb stadium before reinforcements arrived to quell the fighting.

Extra police and firemen using high pressure waterguns finally quelled yesterday's outbreak in which dozens of people were injured, some seriously.

A witness said hundreds of Red Star Belgrade fans were still detained at the stadium three hours after the riot in which fans threw stones and punched and kicked their rivals.

Zagreb television earlier showed opposing supporters of the Red Star and Dinamo Zagreb teams breaking through partition fences and invading the pitch from several sides of the Dinamo stadium.

Doctors in Zagreb's two main hospitals said at least 37 people, including 13 policemen, were injured, three critically.

The end-of-season match was cancelled after the rioting broke out an hour before the scheduled kick-off.

Zagreb police refused to say how many fans were arrested but the television showed dozens being pushed into police vans.

Dinamo fans had predicted clashes with the Red Star supporters because Dinamo had failed to win the first division league championship.

Police are driven back

48

THE Mirror

Thursday, May 30, 1985 **FORWARD WITH BRITAIN** ★ 18p

42 DEAD

Cup Final horror toll

CARNAGE: A woman stands amid a pile of bodies outside the stadium in Brussels.

AT least 42 Italian and Belgian soccer fans were crushed and trampled to death in a drink-crazed battle with Liverpool supporters last night.

And it is feared the final death toll could reach 60.

This was the blackest day yet for English soccer whose fans already have the worst reputation in Europe.

The disaster at the European Cup final in Brussels between Liverpool and Juventus was an horrific climax to the most tragic soccer season for years.

Millions watched worldwide as riots broke out between rival supporters before the match.

Prime Minister Margaret Thatcher watched the violence on TV with horror.

She said: "Those responsible have brought shame and dishonour to the community and to football."

She ordered an immediate report from British Embassy staff in Brussels.

It was a tragic end to the career of Liverpool manager Joe Fagan, who had earlier announced that he would retire after last night's match.

At the height of the trouble he went to the stands wearing a Liverpool team shirt to appeal for calm.

And Juventus players also came onto the pitch in an attempt to defuse the situation.

The violence, the worst in European soccer

Margaret Baskott

DISTRAUGHT mum Margaret Baskott phones Brussels from Liverpool supporters' club to find out if her sons Ian and Gary are safe.

If YOU are worried about a friend or relative who went to the match this is the emergency number to ring . . .

051-709-6010

history, started when Liverpool fans commandeered a large section of the ground reserved for Italians.

FRIGHTENED Juventus fans were pinned back, causing concrete barriers to collapse.

Thousands of sup-

Turn to Page Two

THE SHAME AND THE ANGUISH — See Pages 2, 3, 4, 5, 14, 15, 26, 27 and 28

WOMEN AND FOOTBALL

Watching football matches is a male dominated pastime. Very little effort has ever been made to question this, let alone do anything about it. The terraces are still rife with blatant sexism and mysogyny. A significant proportion of football supporters actually want a women-free space, supposedly to get away from their partners with the 'lads'.

The role of women in football has largely been limited to selling refreshments in the kiosks, working in club shops and the grotesque spectacle of scantily clad women presenting an award, advertising some of the sponsors' products or posing for pictures on the pitch, roared on by thousands of baying men yelling, "Get your tits out for the lads".

Football grounds are one of the last bastions of a male dominated society, where boasts of the latest 'cop off' are fuelled by an attitude that women are only fit for housework and sex. This all contributes to the intimidating atmosphere apparent to many at grounds. For a woman, football can be an embarassing and humiliating experience.

Football has never been a family outing, despite what some of the media try to make out, and women have only ever made up a small proportion of the crowds. The popular scenario for women who do attend is that they have been dragged along unwillingly by boyfriends or husbands, usually as a one-off occasion to show the 'other half' what it's all about. This may be true in a number of cases, but the important fact is that an increasing number of devoted fans are women, who are certainly not ignorant of the intricacies of the game and could put some of their male counterparts to shame in loyalty and knowledge of their club. In fact, the fanaticism of women supporters must be massive if they are prepared to put up with the lousy conditions faced by all fans and the obstacle of sexist language all around them. The real tragedy is that a lot of women are interested in football, but are discouraged from attending matches because of the aggressive and macho atmosphere or because they are told it is not the done thing for women to be football fans by parents or friends. Football is such a staggering experience that it should cut across all races, sexes, ages and physical disability.

In January 1990, the World in Action programme, 'Send for the sisters' was broadcast on I.T.V. The programme was an analysis of women and football, and the concept that women could play a role in solving football's ills. Rather embarassingly, the programme featured a group of Stockport County fans who declared that women had no place in football and that they should not in future. The interviewees appeared to have been hand-picked to represent the stereotypical image of the male, sexist, coarse and macho fan. This sort of irresponsible and unproductive journalism has done football supporters no favours in their efforts to shatter the myth that all fans are like this. The fact is that there are women watching football matches who are NOT dragged along by husbands and boyfriends. A lot of young (and older) males are happy to see women on the terraces and do not share the blatant sexist attitiudes of their colleagues.

A particularly sad aspect of women and football is the way in which a number of politicians, sociologists, club officials and media have suggested that women should be introduced to football as a calming influence on the excitable, younger males. Sociologist Patrick Murphy of Leicester University's Centre for Football Research declared that, "Football in this country is predominantly a male preserve - possibly one of the most attractive features of the game to football hooligans. I think an influx of females would undermine this masculine imagery and change the atmosphere at matches". However, football hooligans are attracted to football because it is exciting and is an opportunity to meet friends, there is certainly an element of machismo in the violence but it is dubious if the presence of women would 'cure' the desire for a punch-up. The term 'an influx of females' is typical of much of the academic garbage emanating from this country. Women are individual people and not some homogeneous block to be sent in to solve a problem. If Murphy means that he wants to see a calmer and more sedate atmosphere, then he is doing as great a disservice to football as the 'law and order brigades' more lunatic calls to ostracise football fans even more. There is a difference between eliminating the fascist elements of soccer crowds and the volatile and exciting atmosphere of the ends. The patronising attitude of so-called experts (usually always men) is more sickening because it is insitutionalised. Women go to football matches because they want to watch the game and enjoy the atmosphere, not out of some sort of social responsibility. In addition, this idea lumps all young males into the easy option pigeon-hole of 'hooligan'.

In addition, one of the arguments put forward by clubs for improving facilities is that it might attract women. It seems that the clubs have identified all women as fussy, comfort loving people, who will undoubtedly want to sit down. But women fans come from all backgrounds and are of diverse ages. Most of those who are football fans are young (though by no means all), are perfectly happy standing and thrive on the terrace lifestyle. The aim should be to treat women as equals - football fans - and not as some sort of alien 'problem' that needs the clubs running round like headless chickens to solve, because of calls to be 'progressive'.

An interesting case is that of St.Pauli, who play in Hamburg, West Germany. For years, this team, based in a working class district of Hamburg, has been supported by thousands of anarchists who live in the squats near to the ground. The fanzine 'Rodney, Rodney' has produced an excellent report on the club and its goalkeeper, who goes on demonstrations in support of the squatters! The article pointed out that about a quarter of St. Pauli's fans are women and that they are just as fanatical about the game as men, "which sheds some light on all this trendy nonsense about needing to sanitise and seat crowds in order to attract 'families' ('Rodney, Rodney', issue 5, P.O.Box 19 (SEPDO) Manchester M12 5RZ).

Of course, this is not to say that everything would be perfect for women if the sexism was tackled. In particular, toilet facilities for women need to be drastically improved - the practical improvements should be easier to tackle than accepted attitudes to women. The women who watch football matches are contributing to challenging the male bastion situation by merely being there and not acting as a sterilising agent. Many fans I have spoken to are realising that the appearance of women is not going to ruin the game and are impressed by their loyalty (loyalty to the club comes before prejudice to many fans). Hence, male fans are slowly starting to treat everyone as fans of 'our' club, regardless of sex. Things have a long way to go, but they are starting to change and surely a positive attitude to tackling sexism in football is better than playing on the loutish minority, with beer guts and sexual hang-ups?

The last few years at Edgeley Park have seen more teenage women on the Popular Side. They have come along with their mates and have latched onto the charged and volatile atmosphere of the

52

terraces. Notions of football spectating not being for females are being thrown aside. For many, the chance to hang around with hundreds of lads of the same age is pretty appealing too!

Part of the reason why women have not attended football matches in large numbers in the past is the attitude of the English to women playing football. In schools, it is rare to see girls encouraged to play football. There are regular stories in the newspapers about talented players being refused the chance to play simply because of their sex. Playing football is an integral part of catching the football bug - if this is repressed then obviously the desire to watch football will be diminished.

In Europe, women's football is not only accepted, but is a major spectator and playing game. In Britain, it is such an unusual phenomenon that the film 'Gregory's Girl' could play on the theme. Most fans in this country probably do not even realise that there is a Women's Football Association with 7,000 registered players. Women's football has been ignored or ridiculed by the media and hindered by the apathy of their male counterparts in the F.A. and Football League. The 'old boys' set up of footballing authorities probably feels threatened by the concept of women playing football.

A particularly encouraging sign has been the increased awareness shown in fanzines about the issue of female fans. There is a proposed women's fanzine called 'Born Kicking' being put together. Hopefully, the reduced violence and moves to improve facilities will contribute to encouraging men and women back to the game. The problem does run deeply into the blatant, ingrained sexism of *some* working class male football supporters and attitudes to women from those running the game - but rather than writing football off as a macho sport, it would be better to involve all in attempting to challenge these concepts so that everyone can enjoy the culture of football.

HILLSBOROUGH

After the Valley Parade fire disaster at Bradford in 1985, in which 56 people died, the subsequent Popplewell Report condemned the state of many grounds and outlawed the lethal, timber based stands. The fire had spread rapidly through the wooden seating due to rubbish that had accumulated under the stand over years of neglect. Many clubs, especially Third and Fourth Division, lost their old stands to the new regulations. Stockport County pulled down their beloved Cheadle End and concreted it over for more terracing (the irony being, that in the wake of the Taylor Report, seating will have to be put in again). What the Popplewell Report ensured was that the likelihood of another Bradford fire happening again was minimalised as much as possible. The horror of watching 56 fans , who supported a Fourth Division side as I did, killed is indescribable. That, just four years later, even more fans should lose their lives in a British football ground borders on the unforgiveable.

Hillsborough is one of the best grounds in the country. This was the 31st semi-final of the F.A.Cup that had taken place there. The F.A.Cup semi-final of the 1988/89 season was between Liverpool and Nottingham Forest. The Liverpool fans were allocated the smaller of the ends because this was felt to be the most accessible for the route from Liverpool, despite the fact that it was obvious that Liverpool would bring more fans.

As kick-off approached on the sunny Saturday 15th April, there were still up to 4,000 Liverpool fans waiting to get through the turnstiles. The terracing was not full immediately before the match. The crushing outside the ground became intense, a police horse was lifted off the ground and the police seemed to have lost control. There had been no filtering of the crowd before they reached the turnstiles, as usually happened. The situation degenerated to such an extent that the police felt obliged to open an external gate to ease the pressure. Subsequent video evidence showed that there was no stampede through this gate, but where there is only admittance through turnstiles the fans are filtered in by the turnstiles, so that they can take their place on the terrace in comfort. But the amount of people going through an open gate

54

is considerably higher than a turnstile, so that the pressure of people trying to reach the terraces as kick-off approached mounted. Poor signposting and a lack of police or stewards directing the fans allowed this late arrival to enter the middle of the terracing on the West Stand en masse. In the dark passageways and steps up to the terracing, dozens of people fell in the crush to see the game, which was about to kick off.

On the pitch, the game started, with most people in the ground unaware of what was happening. As the crush intensified, several fans tried to climb the steep and inward turning perimeter fence, but were pushed back by the police who seemed to think it was a pitch invasion. The horror was compounded by the fact that the crush was only in the terracing behind the goal and the rest of the terraces at that end were not even full.

Even after the police realised that something was wrong, they seemed uncertain as to what to do. Many of the police were lined up along the half-way line to separate the fans spilling onto the pitch from the Leppings Lane end from the bemused Forest fans. It was left to those Liverpool fans who had got over the fence to drag others over and to break up advertising boards as makeshift stretchers. The perimeter fences that had been put up to keep the fans off the pitch were to be a major factor in their deaths.

It is pointless to recount the further heartbreaking events of that day. 94 people lay dead by the Saturday night, with a 95th dying later. The glaring fact was that the biggest problem in soccer was not hooliganism any more, but the complacency of those running the game. The causes of the disaster and the events of the following week are of great significance to all soccer fans.

The treatment of fans as a problem, rather than as paying customers, had led to many grounds being turned into fortresses. The fences around pitches went up at many grounds as the most obvious solution to a particular problem, that of pitch invasions. Hooliganism was not eliminated by fences and many of the worst outbreaks of soccer violence in the 1980s were at grounds where there was perimeter fencing. It had been pointed out that the fences could hinder an evacuation of a ground in an emergency, many people pointed out that the Bradford fire would have claimed even more lives if there had been a high perimeter fence to climb. However, the main problem of the fences was that the gates in them were too few and too narrow, the inward turning top to the fences made it impossible for all but the fittest to scale and there was a failure on the part of police and stewards to recognise the pressure on it. In addition, the crush barriers were themselves mangled under the pressure of the fans.

The stereotyping of football fans meant that the police immediately jumped to the conclusion that there was a pitch invasion and even when those escaping screamed what was happening, they were ignored as usual.

Policing, stewarding and the operations of the emergency services were all slow to react and it seemed that no contingency plans were being put into action. The police had trouble explaining to the emergency services what was happening, and even where it was happening. The lack of emergency and medical facilities horrified both Glyn Phillips, a G.P. who was injured at Hillsborough, and John Ashton, senior lecturer in community medicine at Liverpool University. There were no defibrillators, used to revive crush victims. An oxygen cylinder was empty. No cutting equipment was available. As alarming to the medically trained observers was the lack of planning and the ensuing chaos.

No P.A. announcements were made, other than calling for plans to clear the pitch. Tannoy announcements could have alerted both fans and police to the extent of the crushing.

It is true that many fans arrived quite late, whether due to delays on the roads from Liverpool or going for a drink before the game (the police had told all coaches to be in Sheffield by midday). Fans traditionally arrive at matches in the last 30 minutes before kick-off, it seems that no-one had appreciated the problems this could cause. On this occasion, there was a higher than usual number of spectators waiting to gain admission close to kick-off and, coupled with the absence of filtering, this led to crushing outside the ground. It is believed that several hundred fans did not have tickets, but this would not have made a great difference if it is true.

In hindsight, the ticket allocation was obviously wrong, but even before the game, many people had pointed out that, as Liverpool were bringing more fans, they should have had the larger of the ends. But, of course, no-one listens to fans.

The promised independent inquiry would highlight the causes of Hillsborough. The week after the disaster was a cauldron of emotions - the mourning of the city of Liverpool for it's dead and an astonishing series of accusations and counter accusations in the media.

Much of Liverpool fell into a sense of shock for the rest of the weekend. A special black fringed edition of the Liverpool Echo was produced on the Sunday, which seemed to bring home the horror of the previous day's events to the people of Liverpool. Services were held throughout the city and country to mourn the dead - there was utter disbelief that a game of football, so used to bringing pleasure to its supporters, could result in a slaughter of innocents.

It is perhaps the clearest indication of the importance football plays in the lives of ordinary people that it united a whole community in grief. The fans' response was to turn Anfield into a sea of flowers as a shrine. By the evening of Monday 17th April 1989, it was estimated that 150,000 had visited the charged atmosphere of Anfield and by the following Sunday the pitch was half full, knee deep, in flowers. The main purpose of this was to allow the pent up frustration, pain and anger out, as anyone could cry openly without worrying that anyone would think of them as soft. The players of Liverpool threw their stardom aside and rallied to help and comfort the fans. Craig Johnstone, a former player, flew from Australia to help. Liverpool closed ranks in a show of mutual support - sadly, this was to be an act of self-defence too.

The outrageous smears were intially started by South York-shire police, who seemed to be going on the offensive to defend their failings, which everyone had seen on television over the weekend. First of all, the police blamed the surge solely on the late arrival of fans from the pubs. The campaign mounted with the Police Federation claiming that their officers were spat on as they were trying to save lives and that many fans were drunk. Paul Middup, the secretary of the South Yorkshire Police Federation, reported that a W.P.C., giving mouth to mouth resusitation, was urinated on.

These accusations , made before an inquiry had been held or a clear picture had emerged, proved to be groundless and were condemned by fans and politicians. Even the Merseyside Police Federation rebuked their South Yorkshire colleagues, their secretary Bill Braben saying, "It is a terrible thing to make allegations like this before proper enquiries have been made". The anger of the relatives of the victims was understandably great. The coroner, a year later, reported that only 15 of the victims had above the legal maximum of alcohol for driving in their blood-streams. Video evidence by the B.B.C. showed no evidence of hooliganism. To be fair, many police officers felt that they were being singled out for blame by the media, but to counter this by scurrilous accusations was unjustifiable.

More hurt was caused by several newspapers, notably the 'Sun' and the 'Daily Star', taking up the drunken yob story as "The Truth" and embellishing it with stories of people stealing from the bodies of the deceased. This brought massive condemnation. Copies of the 'Sun' were publicly burnt in Liverpool and newsagents either refused to sell it or reported sales as minimal. Anger against the paper still lingers in Liverpool.

Perhaps less predictable were the comments of Jacques Georges, the French president of UEFA, that the Liverpool fans were like 'beasts'. The English football fan is tarnished with such a reputation that a high ranking international official jumped to the conclusion that 95 dead English fans should automatically be equated with hooliganism, before he knew any of the facts.

Allegations of drunkenness were initially fuelled by publicans stating that Liverpool fans had damaged their property and drank their pubs dry. One of these, a Mr. Ollenshaw, was initially reported as saying, "The pub was packed. We had an extremely busy day. They weren't buying halves and pints, they were buying crates and taking them outside". The following day, he retracted his statement and it transpired that most of the fans in his pub were Nottingham Forest fans. Ollenshaw claimed that journalists had put the words in his mouth.

A year later, and even after the final inquiry had been published, Peter Wright of the South Yorkshire police was still declaring that the Liverpool fans were drunk and aggressive. Wright pointed out that his officers had suffered stress in the wake of Hillsborough, almost as if this was more important than the fact that 95 people had lost their lives. This is not to say that officers have not faced a great deal of trauma, but it is important to put this into perspective.

Many fans still felt helpless in the face of police and media allegations that they knew to be false. Fortunately, other parts of the media were more supportive. The accusations were countered by the supporters' club, the fans themselves and, perhaps most effectively, by Rogan Taylor of the Football Supporters Association who spoke with clarity, calm and conviction. Taylor urged all parties to avoid apportioning blame and that West Midlands police should be allowed to gather information for the inquiry without the added burden of recriminations being hurled around.

Much has been written, and there is doubtless more to come, about the events of 15th April 1989 and its aftermath. The impact on the lives of all soccer fans, regardless of their allegiance, of Hillsborough has yet to see its full significance. In the wake of Hillsborough, for once, football seemed irrelevant for a short time. The consciousness of soccer fans was highlighted in the show of respect and solidarity made by other clubs and their fans. All games in the following week had a minutes silence, which was deafening in its message of sympathy. This was the truth of Hillsborough, not the lurid newspaper articles. The most fitting epitaph would be an upheaval in the way that fans are treated, and their safety becoming more important than profit.

THE TAYLOR REPORT

The inquiry into the Hillsborough disaster was carried out by the Rt. Hon. Lord Justice Taylor, with evidence gathered by the West Midlands police force. There was understandable suspicion, felt by many fans, of one police force gathering information that could be critical of another police force. To add to this, the press and West Yorkshire police had come up with lurid stories of Liverpool fans being drunk and stealing from dead bodies. Hence, Taylor had to formulate an accurate report from a background of accusations and counter accusations.

Taylor's report was the ninth official report into soccer's problems and he stated from the start that there is no point holding inquiries unless the recommendations are actually acted upon. In his research, Taylor visited a large number of grounds and was alarmed by the complacency that existed, even after Hillsborough, with the "It couldn't happen here" syndrome rife.

The 109 page final report on 'The Hillsborough Stadium Disaster' was published in January 1990. Most people considered it to be an excellent report, which had accurately assessed the events of 15th April 1989. The report was more than just another inquiry into a football disaster or outbreak of hooliganism. The recommendations, if acted upon, would alter the whole culture of spectating at football matches. The report was an analysis of the 'blight of football', which Taylor identified as being old grounds, poor facilities, hooliganism, excessive drinking and poor leadership.

The significance of the report could be great, the following is a synopsis of the Final Recommendations:-

1 - 4: There should be all seated accomodation in First and Second Division clubs in England, and the Premier Division in Scotland, by the 1994/5 season (1993/4 for 'high risk' games) to be achieved by a 20% reduction in standing capacity each year from August 1990. By the 1999/2000 season, all-seating would be necessary for all sports grounds designated under the Safety of Sports Grounds Act 1975, to be achieved by a 10% annual reduction in the standing capacity.

5: An Advisory Design Council should be established to

disseminate and research information on football stadia design.

6: The Footballing Licensing authority should have the power to review the discharge of functions by the local authority.

7 - 10: Maximum capacities for terraces. The Safety Certificate should specify the maximum number of spectators per pen or area, which would be limited by tickets, counting etc. The maximum capacity should be in accordance with the Green Guide figures. When the maximum capacity is reached in a pen, that pen should be closed off. The maximum number of spectators coming through a turnstile should be 660/hour and not the present figure of 750/hour.

11 - 12: Filling and monitoring the terraces. Police and clubs should arrange their respective functions in relation to crowd control and safety, in writing. There should be a steward or police officer on the pitch, solely to monitor each pen, if the area is over a third full or holds 2,000 people, whichever is the lowest.

13: Gangways should be kept clear and painted a conspicuous colour.

14 - 21: Spikes or inward turning fences should be removed. Perimeter fences should be a maximum of 2.2 metres high, with sufficient gates of a minimum width of 1.1 metres. Gates should be painted in distinctive colours for identification and kept unlocked with an attendant police officer or steward. Stewards and police officers should be trained to recognise crowd densities, signs of distress and crowd dynamics. Cutting equipment and a clear indication of who was to use it should be available, the decision to use it being made by the senior police officer at the ground.

22 - 23: Crush barriers should be replaced on the first sign of significant degrees of corrosion. The layout of barriers should be reviewed so that it complies with the Green Guide.

24 - 31: Safety Certificates should make mandatory the criteria in the Green Guide. All Safety Certificates should be reviewed by the relevant local authority annually and the criteria for issuing such certificates be reviewed with the aid of an Advisory Group comprised of all relevant bodies.

32 - 43: Taylor outlines the duties of the football club. He expects them regularly to inspect and monitor the capacity of the turnstiles, all the spectators in one area of the ground should be able to pass through the turnstiles supplying that area in one hour. Closed circuit T.V. should monitor the density of crowds. Signposting should be clear and relevant. Information of tickets should

be unambiguous and information requesting that spectators be in position by a certain time should corrolate with planned crowd control arrangements. A record of ticket sales before a match should be kept on computer, while all-ticket matches should be confined to those games where a capacity crowd is expected. Taylor urged the clubs to liaise with supporters' clubs over pre-match entertainment to encourage people to arrive early. Stewards should be fit, trained and be present in sufficient numbers. The club has a duty to provide a police room of sufficient size for officers and equipment, with a view of the whole ground.

44 - 53: Police planning. The Chief Constable of each police force should nominate a chief officer to liaise with each lub and local authority over safety. The importance of overcrowding should be stressed at police pre-match briefings. Arrest procedures should be reviewed so that an arresting officer is kept from his/her post for the minimum of time. The option of postponing kick-offs should be at the discretion of the commanding police officer, Taylor recommends that 'high risk' matches be considered for early kick-offs or a Sunday fixture. Data on crowd density should be available, with officers skilled in its interpretation. Police authorities should review the charges they make for policing so that it is realistic, the Home Office should ensure consistency of practice.

54 - 58: Communications. Sufficient police communication systems should be available so that there would be no over-crowding of airwaves, with a separate channel for the Police Commander. Land lines between the control room and key parts of the ground should complement radio communications. Within the control room, there should be a public address system for inside and outside the ground, with a recognisable signal to precede announcements.

59 - 63: Co-ordination of emergency services. Police, fire and ambulance services should liaise over safety at each ground. Police must give fire and ambulance services full details of matches, routes of entry and exit and any difficulties. Lines of communication should always be kept free between the control room and the emergency services. Contingency plans for access for emergency vehicles should be thoroughly laid down.

64 - 69: First aid, medical facilities and ambulances. There should be one trained first aider per 1,000 spectators, with one or more first aid rooms equipped with professional advice and made part of the Safety Certificate. A medical practitioner should be

63

present at all games with over 2,000 spectators and a fully equipped ambulance should be in attendance at all games with an expected crowd of over 5,000. The Safety Certificate should specify the number of ambulances to be present and, at matches with over 25,000 spectators, a 'major incident equipment vehicle' capable of attending to 50 casualties should be deployed in addition to the ambulances.

70 - 73: Offences and penalties. Consideration should be given to creating an offence of selling tickets on match days without the club's authority. The following should be made a specific offence i)throwing a missile, ii)chanting obscene or racialist abuse, iii)going onto the pitch without reasonable excuse. Taylor suggests giving attendance orders on match days for those convicted of football related offences and that electronic tagging be considered.

74 - 76: The Green Guide should be reviewed in accordance with this report, with special emphasis on crush barriers.

If the above recommendations are actually acted on - and it must be remembered that the usual reaction to inquiries has been to say how important they are, and to conveniently forget them - the football fan standing on the terraces could see his/her world turned upside down.

Many of the suggestions are for things which have been obvious to soccer fans for years, but have either been overlooked or ignored by the authorities. The concept of maximum capacities for terraces is welcome and would make big games much more comfortable and safe. Also, for the fans, the recommendations relating to fences, gates and crush barriers will certainly be welcomed in the light of Hillsborough. The review of Safety Certificates and the importance laid on the already operative Green Guide guidelines on safety at sport stadiums are perfectly logical and there is no reason why this cannot be acted on immediately.

Much of the report is made up of responses to specific failings on the day of the disaster - such as pressure on the turnstiles, a breakdown in the hierarchy and communication of the police, a failure to make P.A. announcements and the slowness in getting medical aid to the victims. All of these things should have been done with the existing organisation patterns, the report should result in ensuring that these failures do not happen again.

The contentious part of the report for football and its related lifestyle is the proposal to remove standing in grounds by as early as 1993 for some First and Second Division clubs. Lord Justice Taylor believes that seating at grounds will make them safer places. It is true that there would be less chance of crushing due to overcrowding, but there could still be crushing outside the grounds and any hooliganism or accident in the rows of seats could make it harder to get away in a panic situation. Seating will not solve hooliganism.

The introduction of all-seating stadia would have a drastic effect on the whole atmosphere of football matches. It is the supporters who make football what it is, and those standing on the terraces make the largest contribution. The whole concept of a football culture is largely dependent on the camaraderie and shared experiences of those massed on the concrete terracing - moves to abolish this haven from the restraints of society are an assault on a traditional working class entertainment. The replacement of this with an American-style squeaky clean all-seated stadia may seem ideal, but it is mooted by those who have no understanding of what it means to be part of an end.

Taylor stated in his report that, "I am not really convinced that the cherished culture of the terraces is wholly lost when fans are seated", which shows his lack of understanding of the fans and the report, excellent as it is, is really aimed at improving the running of football and not the culture of its followers. It should be possible to ensure the safety of all fans, whether standing or sitting, if the rest of the recommendations are acted upon. A reduction in the capacity of terraces is a legitimate policy in the light of Hillsborough and many other crushes which have not resulted in fatalities (and hence could be conveniently ignored). However, monitoring and maximum capacities would ensure safety and comfort, while not detracting from the atmosphere.

Most of the media supported Taylor's proposals for an all-seated stadia, while acknowledging the nostalgia of the terraces. What the hacks in the press box fail to grasp is that nostalgia and tradition are an integral part of watching league football and an integral part of working class culture - this is not being bogged down in the past, but a fact which is important for future developments in football.

The failures that led to Hillsborough were largely of the organisation of football, the design of grounds, the safety hazards caused by fences and barriers, lack of communication of the situation to other fans and police etc. - because of this, it is suggested that the solution is to simply remove the terraces altogether. Fans died because of mistakes by the authorities and now will lose their right to stand at matches because of this.

For matches where there is no likelihood of a maximum capacity or overcrowding, such as most Second, Third and Fourth Division clubs in England and most First and Second Division teams in Scotland, the removal of terracing would be pointless. If people feel so strongly about sitting at matches, there is nothing stopping them at present. If the safety measures urged by Taylor are implemented then there is no reason why smaller clubs, at least, should not be able to retain the terracing.

For the Taylor Report to have any real impact, the whole attitude of the clubs, police and football authorities towards spectators must change. While fans are still turnstile fodder to many clubs and the scum of the earth to the police, the problems will continue in one form or another.

Most of the recommendations would not cost a great deal of money, but would call for a change in priorities and responsibility. However, the cost of all-seated stadia would be enormous in both construction costs and reduced capacities (unless more people were attracted to smaller clubs due to improved facilities). Of course, many grounds are in a shabby condition, are cramped and badly situated in residential areas. 58 of the English League grounds were built before 1910! It has been suggested that the cost of implementing the Taylor Report could be £130 million. There seems to be logic in the politicians pointing out that many clubs spend vast amounts of money on transfer fees and little on the facilities for their fans. There is a Catch-22 situation here for the fans want safer grounds and better facilities, but perhaps even more want success, which usually means buying players. The clubs come under immense pressure to buy players and the irony is that if a club does not spend, then the gates fall so that safety is more easily achieved - and if the club does spend vast sums on players, then crowds increase but there is little money to spend on the ground, in the short term at least. In the wake of the Taylor Report, the Home Secretary, David Waddington, said that costs incurred would have to be borne out by the clubs, regardless of the fact that this could put small clubs out of business. One of the newest clubs in the League is the Glanford Park stadium at Scunthorpe, which is a purpose built stadium built out of the town centre, with plenty of parking space and good facilities. However, the ground is outdated already because Scunthorpe's fans did not mind the move from the Old Showground, but insisted on being allowed to stand, so all that will have to change.

Larger clubs may have found the money, but the smaller clubs would really struggle. The lifeline came in the unlikely form of John Major's budget of 1990, in which the tax levied on pools betting was reduced to release £100 million over five years for ground improvements.

Although not in the Final Recommendations, Taylor was disparaging of the facilities in most grounds and the treatment of fans, "No-one would expect, or indeed want, plush carpeting or haute cuisine when visiting the terraces, but accomodation and facilities have often been below the basic decent standard necessary to give spectators dignity let alone comfort".

Taylor summed up the problem of hooliganism well, "I know of no other sport or establishment in a civilised country in which it is necessary to keep those attending from attacking each other", but apart from suggesting that further specific offences be created and that electronic tagging be introduced, he fails to grasp what hooliganism is about or to put foreward any new solutions, preferring to take the moral high ground. Few people in authority seem to realise that violence is a release of pent up frustration and hooliganism is also a good laugh to those involved.

A Mori poll in a report, 'The Missing Voice', commissioned by the Football League, and issued after the Taylor Report (though carried out before it) gave an interesting insight into the wishes of the fans. Better toilet and refreshment facilities, pre-match and half-time entertainment, a free Football League magazine and a voluntary membership scheme if it covered free admission to local leisure facilities, were all high up the list of priorities. The poll showed that most supporters who now stand at matches, want to continue to be able to do so and this is most strongly felt in lower division clubs.

Taylor's report did end one proposed solution to soccer's ills that had been in the news for at least the previous year - that of compulsory I.D. cards.

68

When Saturday Comes

The Half Decent FOOTBALL Magazine

March 1990 No. 37

60p

The Future Of Football....

69

THE GREAT I.D. CARD FIASCO

From the Heysel disaster onwards, the government had informed the football authorities that if they did not put their own house in order, mainly over the question of hooliganism and not safety, then the government would take steps to do it for them. Inevitably, the buck-passing continued, apathy reigned and the government introduced the Football Spectators Bill. Part of this bill included the introduction of compulsory identity cards for all fans attending football matches.

The compulsory I.D.card was seized on by the government as the cure to all football's ills. Despite the fact that no-one at Westminster seemed to have thought the issue through or considered any potential problems, the scheme was championed by the Prime Minister and the Minister for Sport, Colin Moynihan.

The first glaring feature of the compulsory scheme is that it was a gross infringement of civil liberties - if you want to watch football, you must carry a card. No other section of society, in this country, has to carry I.D. cards around and the very idea alienated decent soccer fans even more. All football fans would be labelled as potential yobs and be reduced to name, number and bar code reading.

Soccer fans campaigned fiercely against I.D. cards. Opposition to the scheme united fans and helped to develop the grass roots consciousness of supporters more than almost any other issue. Public meetings were held, M.P.s were bombarded with objections and banners appeared at grounds saying 'No to I.D. Cards'. Colin Moynihan was singled out as the main target for the fury, his home address was published, the fanzines ranted and he even received sackfuls of death threats and parcels carrying excrement. Other schemes had been introduced, which may appear to be intrusive, such as searches at turnstiles and C.C.T.V. - but there was little objection to these because the reason for carrying them out could be clearly seen. Football fans saw compulsory I.D. cards as dangerous, unfair and totally irrational, and they finally found their voice to oppose them.

The National Council for Civil Liberties joined the campaign when it was realised that the government intended to use 'smart cards', some of which can be read in the holder's pocket without that person knowing. An article in 'The New Scientist', 4th February 1989, suggested that the Football Spectators Bill gave no clear indication as to the rights of the holder and that one of the favourites for the lucrative contracts, that of G.E.C., could hold 5,000 characters of text - the equivalent of several A4 pages of information.

In practice, the scheme would simply not work. If there was to be a technical fault in the computer at just one turnstile, chaos would quickly follow. The likelihood of a computerised system that would never fail was slim, to say the least. In addition, the whole thing could provide the hooligan with a new game - sabotage the turnstiles.

In the 15 minutes before any match, there is a build up of fans outside most grounds. The need to get people quickly through the turnstiles is paramount, the results of this not happening contribute to events such as Hillsborough. Having to show a card or run it through a computer would undoubtedly slow this process up drastically and the potential for crushing as the kick-off approached would be enormous.

The police were also against the scheme as it stood and were particularly alarmed at the queues that would form. The Chief Constables told Taylor, "All our experience has been that the computer salesmen had offered much and delivered little. The consequences of repeated failure, hostile queues and endless delay are unthinkable".

Attendances would fall drastically if every fan had to have a card to get into the game because those fans who just attend a few games a year, or decide to attend a game at the last minute (if they were on holiday or visiting a town where an interesting match was on, for instance), would not be able to get in. For some clubs, the casual crowd is a significant proportion of their attendances and the elimination of this support could spell financial disaster. Hence, most clubs were against the compulsory card scheme.

Luton Town introduced a compulsory card scheme after the riot at the Luton vs. Millwall game. However, in their successful 1987/8 season, attendances fell by 22%. Arrests have been almost non-existant, but several other clubs have also had hardly any arrests, without membership schemes. Also, away fans can gain admittance, if they really want to, by obtaining a membership card a few days before a match.

The irony is that the I.D. card scheme was being mooted at a time when hooliganism inside grounds was declining rapidly and arrests were also falling. Incidents of terrace violence still appear on the news occasionally, but this is because it makes good T.V. if it is exaggerated and the absence of large scale disorder makes even minor incidents stand out.

The compulsory membership scheme was based on the premise that if a fan was arrested and convicted, their card would be confiscated so that that fan would be unable to attend future games. Of course, attendance orders at police stations would achieve exactly the same thing and not oppress peaceful fans. Another point that was overlooked is that the dedicated football hooligans do not get caught very often, rarely fight inside grounds any more and are quite intelligent enough to use someone else's card to enter a ground. The I.D. card, in any case, does not prevent trouble, it merely attempts to prevent the same people from doing it again, if they are convicted.

To prevent fraud or transfer, the I.D. card would have to have a photograph because, as John Duncan in 'When Saturday Comes' pointed out, "This means that any system will have to incorporate mechanical (computer) checking and visual checking of cards. Otherwise, there is no point in having the photo, which a computer cannot recognise".

Despite this weight of opposition, and even in the wake of Hillsborough, the Prime Minister pressed ahead with the I.D. card scheme and the second reading, on 31st October 1989, passed throught the Commons with only a handful of Tories rebelling.

In the end, it was Lord Justice Taylor who, fortunately, was prepared to listen to the arguments of experts and fans. He declared that the scheme was not only an affront to civil liberties, it was also an administrative nightmare that was technologically infeasible. The government remained stubborn and refused to admit its almighty blunder, but the scheme was quietly dropped - although it still remains on the statute books in case it is ever needed. Soccer fans must be aware of the last point, but also take a well deserved bow in their organised efforts to force the abandonment of such a ludicrous idea.

FOOTBALL FANS ANSWER BACK

One of the most encouraging and welcome developments for soccer fans has been the development of the Football Supporters Association. The F.S.A. was launched on Merseyside in 1985. The Association emerged in the wake of the Heysel disaster, within 12 months there were seven regional branches and the first national conference was held in May 1986. In 1990, there are 21 regional branches and affiliated groups in colleges.

The F.S.A. organisation is in three tiers. There is a management committee of five national officers and five elected members. Secondly, there is a national council of five national officers and one representative from each of the regional branches. Finally, the 21 regional branches each have their own committees of elected officers.

The regional officers are particularly interesting as they contain all the mebers in their area. They bring supporters of different clubs together to meet regularly and develop policies for all the fans, which helps to break down the traditional barriers between different sets of fans.

The F.S.A. states its aims as:

1) To gain representation for football supporters on the executive bodies which control football.

2) To provide an independent and democratic structure through which the views of football supporters may be channelled and articulated.

3) To promote the game of football and to provide goodwill between football supporters.

4) To promote and initiate campaigns on issues of concern to football supporters. Particularly to campaign for improved facilities for disabled supporters and women.

5) To carry out research into, and to disseminate information on, football related issues.

6) To oppose racism, sexism and sectarianism in football.

The F.S.A. has carried out surveys on the facilities and amenities in grounds and has sent representatives to the regional safety advisory groups set up by Lord Justice Taylor.

Another important achievement by the F.S.A. has been to be

73

represented on the Supporters Liaison Committee with the F.A. and the League, and area meetings with club management.

Obviously, progress has been slow for the F.S.A. because of the years of intransigence and of being totally ignored by the clubs and football authorities. The following is an article, 'Reclaiming the game' by Rogan Taylor, which indicates the rise of the F.S.A. and the suspicion and unhelpful attitude it encountered in its first three years of existance:

"As the dead bodies were stacked onto the pitch of the Heysel stadium in 1985, I sat at home watching it all on T.V. As a Liverpool fan who'd witnessed the other great European triumphs of my team, I should have been there - but I couldn't get a ticket.

The champagne was in the fridge at the ready; my kids beside me by the fire but, instead of the match, the purple-faced corpses hypnotised me from the screen. Two months later, the F.S.A. was born.

Like a gazelle birthed on the move, the F.S.A. was running before its feet hit the ground. Supporters all over Britain responded with an energy and commitment to a call to organise and seek proper representation at all levels of the game. Before the end of the season, eight regional branches had been formed and nearly 2,000 members recruited. The first national, campaigning grass roots organisation, open to individual supporters regardless of their club loyalties, called on the F.A. and the Football League to open a dialogue with the fans. The silence was deafening.

What the F.S.A. proposed was, and still is, a revolution in football's hierarchy. Like all revolutions, without the wind of history blowing in your favour, you've got no chance of success. But the wind blew our way. In the Autumn of 1986, the government demanded that football "put its own house in order", or it would do the job itself. Compulsory membership schemes were mooted; banning all away supporters from matches was another possibility. Deep gloom set in at the Football League H.Q.

The League's Anti-Hooligan Committee was set up to prepare a report for submission to Downing Street. As the first twinges of cardiac arrest were felt, the League reached for the panic button. "We need the supporters on our side", they panicked, "Who can mobilise groundswell opinion against compulsory schemes? Who will badger M.P.s? Call for the F.S.A.!". It was the first clear indication that the deeper the crisis, the better our chances of involvement. Only in extremes would the football authorities even consider involving the turnstile-fodder, who feed a mere £60 million a year into the game.

Myself and Peter Garrett (then national secretary) were summoned to the Anti-Hooly Committee meeting at Old Trafford in November. We arrived prepared and presented a document, 'Football Supporters Against Hooliganism', calling for a radical, positive programme which would generally involve fans in devising solutions and democratise decision-making at all levels. Once again, the silence was deafening. The League' report emerged with no mention of any of the proposals we had put forward. (There was a brief line which said that the F.S.A. opposed compulsory schemes!) The report was a pathetic and poorly assembled affair, calling for heavy punishments for 'offenders' and offering the sop of the current 50% membership scheme. The League even congratulated itself on the rapid imposition of CCTV - without even crediting the Football Trust for providing all the money.

Within months, the F.S.A. showed what it could do in the real task of defending supporters' interests. In the spring of 1987, when Q.P.R. fans woke up one Friday morning to find they now supported a team called 'Fulham Park Rangers' (and Wimbledon were planning to merge with Crystal Palace), the London branch sprang into action. They took the merger-moving millionaire Bulstrode by the horns and rapidly formed the Football in London Action Group (FLAG). In Hammersmith Town hall, over 2,000 fans representing half a dozen West London clubs attended a meeting chaired by their F.S.A. London Branch chair, Craig Brewin. Craig led a platform that included P.F.A. leaders, Taylor and Batson, Jimmy Hill, Roy Hattersley, Malcolm McDonald and Gordon Prentice, leader of Hammersmith and Fulham council. Our strategy had been to use the sympathy for Fulham generated by the council and the media to assist the campaigns of other affected clubs and to bring together their fans in a united campaign. It worked. The proposed merger collapsed like a house of cards. London fans saw the potential of a supporters' organisation, independent of all clubs, capable of swift and effective action.

That same spring, the F.S.A. presented a 15,000 signature petition and a dossier of complaints to the F.A. at Lancaster Gate. The petition called on the F.A. to change the ticket allocation system for the Cup finalists, so that genuine fans should get more of them. The dossier detailed and evidenced a wide range of malpractice at Wembley - from policing and stewarding to poor amenities (particularly for disabled fans), and refreshment provision of the lowest order. Copies of the dossier were also sent to Wembley Stadium Ltd. and the Metropolitan Police. Within weeks the police and Wembley responded, leading to a series of contructive meetings. From the F.A.? Yes, you've guessed it - a deafening silence.

We did not even receive a compliments slip from the F.A. We waited six months before writing to ask if any action was forthcoming. We received, in reply, a whitewash letter completely ignoring our dossier and mentioning briefly that the F.A. ticket allocation system was permanently 'under review'!"

The F.S.A. has been at the forefront of the campaigns set up to oppose the plague of proposed takeovers, sales and redevelopments of football grounds which have proliferated in the late 1980s.

The compulsory identity card, championed by Margaret Thatcher and Colin Moynihan, was bitterly opposed by the F.S.A., among other groups. The F.S.A. demanded to be part of any working party that would lead to legislation relating to football.

Of course, the compulsory I.D. card scheme was finally destroyed by the criticisms in the Taylor Report, but it is important to bear in mind that this was the first in which football supporters had any say.

Rogan Taylor became a household figure in April 1989, in the wake of the Hillsborough disaster. As the articulate voice of the Liverpool fans, he had to counter the lies of the media and the police. The F.S.A. came of age through these tragic events, perhaps such opportunities for fans to have their say may yet prevent more suffering, but football still has a long way to go yet.

The F.S.A. is a national body and a great deal of work is done by the supporters' clubs of individual teams and there is a growing awareness of their role in pressing for improvements and a better deal for the fans.

To highlight the need for a grass roots organisation for football fans, on the eve of the World Cup, a domestic incident overshadowed the build up. The Football League relegated Swindon Town from the First to the Third Division after the club was found guilty of financial irregularities. The sickening thing was that the main culprits, ex-Chairman Brian Hillier and ex-manager Lou Macari, who had bet on Swindon losing an F.A. Cup tie against

Newcastle, had already left the club. The fans , who only 10 days earlier had been celebrating the promotion to the First Division for the first time in their history, saw their world fall apart because of the actions of those running the club. The incident sums up British football, rotten to the core and fans having no control over what happens to their game.

And just to make sure that it was not only Swindon's fans who suffered, the Football League waited a week before announcing who would take their place, so that Sheffield Wednesday (the last to be relegated from the First Division), Sunderland (losers of the final of the Second Division play-offs) and Newcastle (who had finished third in the Second Division) were left biting their nails to see who would have the First Division place. To add to this, Bournemouth and Tranmere were left waiting to see who would take the extra place in the Second Division. Amazingly, the decision to promote Sunderland and Tranmere was made before Swindon had appealed and before a proposed High court hearing. On appeal, Swindon were allowed to stay in the Second Division, so Tranmere saw their short-lived euphoria demolished as they had to stay in the Third Division. The contempt for the feelings of the fans by the footballing authorities and the need for a revolution by the fans to take control of their game had never been more obvious.

At the same time in Scotland, Hibernian fans were up in arms over a proposed takeover by arch-rivals Heart of Midlothian. The bid could mean the end of Hibs and the sale of Easter Road. The board executives of both clubs were justifiably the focus of the fans' anger. Ian Young, of the Hibs' supporters club, summed it up by saying, "It's about property speculation, not football. It's a working class game and these city whizz kids don't care if they destroy it".

Until the mid 1980s, virtually the only way that fans could express their opinions about their team was via the supporters' clubs or individual letters to local newspapers.

The supporters' clubs are closely linked to the football clubs, frequently being set up by the clubs to encourage support. The majority of clubs have been intolerant of any criticism emanating from 'their' supporters' clubs. Because of the influence held by the clubs in providing the fans with accomodation, finance etc., the supporters' clubs have tended to be acquiescent groups whose function has largely been limited to providing travel to away games and social functions. The supporters' clubs' loyalty to the club has meant that any suggestions or criticisms have been stifled from within or ignored by the clubs. The idea that fans will turn up in all weathers, to stand in pre-war grounds and watch defeat after defeat without a moan or groan, has been taken by the clubs as the accepted norm - anything that deviates from this is labelled as lack of loyalty and tantamount to revolution.

Of course, it is nothing to do with lack of loyalty, rather that the fans do have the best interests of the club at heart and, as they are the largest single contributor of money to the clubs, they are entitled to have a say in the running of THEIR team. If the club is being run into the ground by a bunch of morons, a true fan will inevitably want to change things, even if this means criticising those running the game.

The main problem is that the best medium for fans to follow the fortunes of their club has been the official match programme, which the club usually has total control over. Some supporters' clubs columns have even been written by club officials and, if written by an ordinary fan, the club can vet articles and there is never a sniff of controversy. Increasingly, a significant number of fans feel out of touch with the team they support and feel helpless and frustrated in having no say. The ivory tower, in which many club officials live, has bred a certain amount of contempt on the terraces. It must be pointed out that this alienation of fans from having a say in the running of their game varies from club to club. Many of the smaller clubs, in particular, have fostered good relations with their fans, but whether this extends to having a voice in the running of the club's affairs is less frequent.

There ARE magazines for football fans, which are general in their coverage, and include such publications as 'Shoot!'. 'Match' and 'Football Monthly'. These are interesting reads, but tend to focus on the footballers and the game itself. The aim of these is to make profit, any controversial material or features on the fans is rare. I was brought up on 'Roy of the Rovers', the football comic which at least featured boardroom struggles, fans' comments and footballers' lives - if only in fictitious cartoon form. The newspapers also carry news of the bigger clubs, but the best 'mainstream' source of information is the Saturday evening football papers of varying colour, size and quality. The queues outside newsagents on Saturdays are testament to this and the letters page is often a rare opportunity for fans to say just what they think of the game.

Between August 1966 and December 1974, the Football League

Review was inserted into most programmes, actually making up the bulk of many. The Review covered the general football scene and it did occasionally contain controversial reading, but finally closed due to financial problems. However, it was not until the appearance of 'Foul' in 1972 that a true alternative football paper first hit the streets, but this was an isolated publication.

The need for organisation at a grass roots level, free from the restrictions of the clubs, came to a head in the 1980s with the two disasters at Bradford and Hillsborough, which were caused largely by the neglect of the safety of the fans. Another development was the spate of proposed ground moves, the property developers sniffing around and merger plans. Charlton moved in with Crystal Palace at Selhurst Park, leaving the Valley behind. There was an astonishing plan to merge Oxford and Reading into one team called Thames Valley Royals. Fulham's Craven Cottage was designated as a block of flats by the developers. Many fans found that their ground, and very team itself, were under threat and that they were seemingly helpless to do anything about it.

An independent voice for the fans had been long sought after, and the late 1980s saw it come in the explosion of the phenomena of football fanzines.

Fanzines are independently produced magazines that are put together by devotees of a particular hobby or pastime. They are frequently produced by only one or a handful of people who are obsessed with their pastime, but have their own ideas on how it should be run. The most notable outbreak of fanzines before the football variety was that associated with punk rock. Punk started out as almost anti-music, as a reaction to the antiseptic music standards of the 1970s and a music industry that showed no interest in anything new, in favour of making mega-bucks out of the bland, established chart orientated stars. Most of the zines were photocopied, badly typed and consisted of reviews and interviews. They gave Punk fans a voice against the powerful music industry. Punk fanzines are still produced in large numbers and it would be fair to say that they have partly influenced the development of football fanzines.

The mid 1980s saw the emergence of a handful of football fanzines, including 'City Gent', the fanzine of Bradford City, York City's 'Terrace Talk' and West Brom's 'Fingerpost'. The general coverage publications followed in 1986, notably 'Off The Ball' and 'When Saturday Comes'. Since then, the fanzines have developed at an astonishing speed, with most clubs now having at least one independent journal.

The important thing about fanzines is that they reflect the HUMOUR of football fans. Having a laugh is a vital part of football culture, whether it be the loud mouthed wag in the crowd (labelled 'The Bloke Behind Me' by 'When Saturday Comes') or travelling to away games with mates. The irreverance shown to those who run the game is hilarious and a major factor in the success story of fanzines.

The titles of the zines have taken on surreal dimensions, such as Gillingham's 'Brian Moore's Head Looks Uncannily Like London Planetarium' or Grimsby's 'Sing When We're Fishing'. Many of the titles only make sense to those who support the team, such as Bournemouth's 'Not the 8502'. It is not just League clubs who have lunatics putting together fanzines, many non-League clubs also have hilarious and excellent quality publications.

Sales of the zines vary from club to club. 'When Saturday Comes' is now distributed by W.H.Smiths, with sales approaching 20,000 per issue. Celtic's 'Not The View' is reputed to sell over 10,000 copies per issue. Most are priced at around 50p, which is cheaper than the official match day programmes.

The contents of the fanzines are generally an irreverant look at football, usually a mixture of the particular team and football in general. Cartoons lie chaotically alongside analytical reviews on the hairstyles of the players or the Greenhouse Effect's impact on the fate of Scottish grounds (in 'The Absolute Game') This bizarre humour helps to take the tension out of traditional rivalries by creating a sense of fun and demolishing the seriousness that some in the game take themselves. The F.A., Football League, government, Colin Moynihan and those running individual clubs are all among the targets of the searing wit of the publications,

In general, the football fanzines reflect and are part of the culture of spectating at football matches, not necessarily unquestioning devotion to the 22 players on the pitch.

Fanzines have also served a more serious function. Some of the best articles on Hillsborough appeared in the independent press, which is logical as they are written by real fans who understand the problems of football because they face the brunt of them. The I.D. card issue was rigorously opposed by the fanzines which demolished the arguments for the scheme with ridicule and biting logic. The various takeover proposals, mergers and threatened ground 'improvements' were also challenged - 'The Voice Of The Valley' and 'The Spur' are examples of fans saying that enough is enough and demanding involvement in the decisions affecting their lives.

A further significance of many of the zines is their anti-racist stance, which is more likely to influence fans than hordes of left-wing students boring everyone silly with a Marxist analysis of race and class. The majority of fans are opposed to the fascist element, but have previously not had the nerve to stand up against the thugs. 'The Orienteer' has a strong anti-racist line, as do other fanzines. 'When Sunday Comes', a Liverpool fanzine, produced an excellent article on John Barnes and racism at Liverpool. Anti-racism incorporated in the general articles has far more impact than a 'racism is wrong' party line. 'Leeds United Against Racism and Fascism' have their own fanzine called 'Marching Altogether', which is doing a lot to counter the influence of the racist element at Elland Road, if unlikely to convert the die-hard fascists themselves.

The directors of football clubs must be having hot flushes seeing publications about the clubs they run and having no control over their content. The fanzines have got up the noses of some clubs to such an extent that they have been banned from some grounds, this happened to Grimsby's 'Sing When We're Fishing' and Boston's 'From Behind Your Fences'. Being a football fan has taken on subversive dimensions for some who revel in winding up the authorities.

The importance of fanzines cannot be overstressed, both from the purely enjoyment side in providing the readership with a good laugh, their role in the developing grass roots consciousness in football and tackling issues that affect all fans, such as I.D. cards, racism, sexism, property developers, the safety and comfort of fans and the impact of the Taylor Report. Phil Shaw, in his book on fanzines, 'Whose Game Is It Anyway', summed up the enigma of football fanzines as, "The message from virtually all these magazines, so varied in quality and allegiance, is clear. It is that football belongs not to television, to an elitist clutch of clubs, to rapacious agents or sensation hungry tabloids, or to the shareholders and sponsors, but to the people whose pounds and partisanship sustain the sport".

The following are fanzines with a general coverage. 'When

Saturday Comes' contains an exhaustive list of all the current fanzines by club:

'The Absolute Game', P.O.Box 303, Southern DO, Edinburgh, EH9 1NE.

'Archie, Archie, What's The Score?', P.O.Box 642, Glasgow G11 7QL.

'Blow Football', 8, Beaumont Road, Bourneville, Birmingham, B30 2DY.

'By Far The Greatest Team', 1, Shire Close, Cowplain, Hants.

'Crazy Horse', Top Floor Studio, 27-29 Union St., London, SE1.

'Dwy Droed Chwith', Encil y Coed, Plasgwyn, Pwllheli, Gwynned, LL53 6UA.

'Each Game As It Comes', 22, Stanley Street, Norton, Stockton on Tees, Cleveland, TS20 1HG.

'Fanzine Monthly', 15/2, Lochend Gdns.,Edinburgh, EH7 6DG.

'Five To Three', P.O.Box 10, Pwllheli, Gwynedd, LL53 5BE.

'The Football Supporter', 59, Oakwood Road, Halewood, Liverpool, L26 1XD.

'Groinstrain', P.O.Box 568, Wimbledon, SW19.

'Hit The Bar', 32, Cecil St.,Blackpool, Lancs, FY1 3RE.

'The Ivor Thirst Good Pub Guide To The Football League', 61,Stratford Rd., West Bridgford, Nottingham.

'The Lad Done Brilliant', 90J St. George's Drive, Pimlico, London, SW1V 4DA.

'Les Bence, Manager's Notes', 5, Clark's Place,Trowbridge, Wilts, BA14 7HA.

'Let's Get Talking', 41, Lockington Avenue, Hartley, Plymouth, Devon, PL3 5QG.

'The Magic Sponge', Snowshine Ltd., Unit 22B, 31 Aire Street, Leeds, LS1 4HT.

'More Than A Game', 56, Springdale Road, Broadstone, Poole, Dorset.

'Non League Football Fanfare', 26, Orchard Road, Kingstone-upon-Thames, Surrey, KT1 2QW.

'On The One Road', P.O.Box 396, Harrow, Middlesex, HA2 9PT.

'Que Sera, Sera, P.O.Box 202, Glasgow. G12 8EQ.

'Rodney, Rodney', P.O.Box 19 (SEPDO) Manchester, M19 5RZ.

'Storming With Menace', 11, Chatsworth Way, Carylon Way, St. Austell, Cornwall, PL25 3SL.

'Tayside Football Review', 45, Sutherland Crescent, Dundee, DD2 2HP.

'Two Left Feet', Encil y Coed, Pwllheli, Gwynedd, LL53 6UA.
'What's The Score', P.O.Box 221, Liverpool, L69 7DD.
'When Saturday Comes', 4th Floor, Pear Tree Court, London, EC1R ODS.

RODNEY, RODNEY!

No. 5

50p

An <u>infrequent</u> Football Fanzine

ZAN - POW - LEE

Exclusive MORRISSEY INTERVIEW

ITALIA '90

The soul of football lies in kids kicking a ball about in the back streets of a British city, on a beach in Brazil or in the deserts of Africa. It is a truly international phenomenon, which is given its climactic expression once every four years in the World Cup finals. Two years of regionalised qualifying matches produced the 24 teams who would make up Italia '90, these included England, Scotland and Ireland.

As soon as Sophia Loren and Luciano Pavarotti had delightfully compered the draw that created a Group F containing England, Holland, Ireland and Egypt, the panic set in. The English and Dutch fans had the most notorious reputations for violence and the fact that this scenario was to be played out on the island of Sardinia was the cherry on the icing on the cake for the gleeful press.

The excitement built up in all the participating countries as the World Cup approached. Millions of people looked forward to the footballing carnival. People who rarely show an interest in football, caught the infectious bug for a month or so in June and July. The usual problem for the British fans of a lack of soccer between May and August was solved by taking their annual holidays in Italy or in front of the T.V.

At the end of the 1989/90 season, there was a notable increase in the wearing of England shirts. Perhaps a more alarming phenomenon was the T-shirts proclaiming aggressive loyalty to England and, to a lesser extent, Scotland, and dire consequences to the rest of Europe. Slogans, usually accompanied by the British bulldog, included 'Brits on the piss', 'We came, we saw, we kicked ass', 'Teargassed in Turin' and 'Italy 1990. Lock up your daughters'. These T-shirts sold like hot cakes.

On a lighter note, the tradition of the England team producing a record for the World Cup continued. However, the difference was that this one was actually good! With the help of New Order, the team got to the top of the charts and got more people interested in the team's performances.

The focus on the fans was, of course, on the potential for violence. The way in which the English supporters forget their tribal loyalties, apart from emblazoning their club's name on flags,

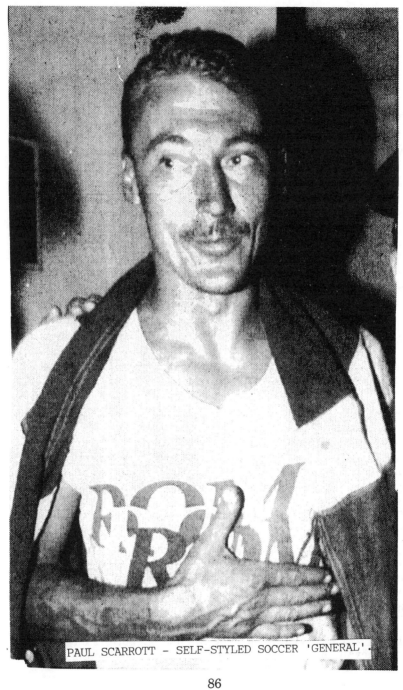

PAUL SCARROTT - SELF-STYLED SOCCER 'GENERAL'.

for the common good of the country is certainly an awe-inspiring prospect. However, the vast majority of the English fans had saved up to go to Italy for a footballing carnival and not a nationalist bloodbath. The media, though, had convinced everyone that trouble was being planned, so that life for the English fans in Italy was going to be difficult.

The press went ga-ga at the potential of the English and Dutch on Sardinia in the same group. The scenarios they conjured up were unbelievable, at best, such as a story that the Italians were planning to attack English fans on the beaches, driving them into the sea and drowning them! The hooligan elements were interviewed and obviously played up to the hacks.

In Italy. press from all over the world sought to photograph a set of Union Jack clad, sieg-heiling fans. A few beers for the 'lads' usually got them their story. The Hitler salute seemed to be an act of defiance, designed to shock onlookers, rather than an allegiance to fascist groups - although this is not to say that there were not elements of these present. The stereotype of the Brits created by T.V., press and authorities is such that locals and police in Sardinia were bound to be edgy and any possibility of everyone having a good time was remote.

Every tiny incident involving English fans was pounced on by the media and blown out of all proportion. Before the tournament had even got under way, two English fans were jailed for 20 days for allegedly stealing a sheet from a hotel room, an occurance that would not warrant a mention in a local paper in England.

The police in Sardinia had been assessing the situation for months and initially declared that they wanted everyone to have a good time, but they would be firm with troublemakers, which sounded fair enough. However, they were presented with horror stories about past English excursions abroad.

In England, the National Football Intelligence Unit (set up after the collapse of trials, following police infiltration of soccer firms) finally got the chance to get on T.V. The Dutch were perceived as the main threat by the N.F.I.U., depite the fact that the evidence was minimal and a Channel 4 news report in the week before had interviewed Dutch fans, who stated that football was on the menu and nothing else. To be fair, the N.F.I.U. did supply names and details of the most notorious English fans to the Italians. This led to one of the most famous yobs, Paul Scarrott, of Nottingham, being expelled from Italy before the World Cup had even started.

Others were turned back later. The N.F.I.U. had no powers to stop fans travelling, but it could pass on information to the Italians, who could refuse them entry to the country.

The trouble with the N.F.I.U., apart from its alarming potential threat to civil liberties, was that it fuelled the image of all fans as having reputations that made the Mafia look like Boy Scouts.

The government again laid the responsibility for behaving at the fans' feet, which meant that they had washed their hands of responsibility, but could use any trouble to bring in more repressive legislation and policing. Colin Moynihan made token trips to Sardinia to try to get alcohol restrictions tightened, which he succeeded in doing. He and the government seemed happy that the Italians had prepared well.

The F.A. also felt obliged to make their own token efforts. They came up with the idea of organising 'official' holidays with tickets included, so that the situation could be monitored by the bureaucrats. The problem was that these tours were often twice the normal price of a normal holiday to Italy. Obviously, most ordinary fans were going to make their own arrangements and, as usual, tickets were easily obtainable in Sardinian banks and shops. The F.A. and ticket allocation have never been a really good mix.

A combination of media reports, N.F.I.U. alarmist information, an onlooking world and the ticket allocation in chaos, contributed to the police deciding to take no messing. The major incident before the game against Holland highlighted this, one missile thrown led to all the England fans being batoned, chased and teargassed in Cagliari. The old problem of innocent fans being on the receiving end of aggressive policing, because of a minority, is the same all over Europe. Why should a fan, walking to a ground, have to suffer tear gas because of the actions of a handful of idiots and police paranoia?

A major element in the tension seemed to be a culture gap between the English and Italians. The Italians were bemused by the drunken antics of noisy English fans. The chanting is harmless, but carried out by sun-burned youths, with cropped hair and draped in national flag, it had the Italians edgy, because they could not understand what was going on. for example, the chant of "Let's go fucking mental" is just another song to the fans, but the police seemed to think the English were going to do just that! In general, there was wariness on both sides (the fact that there were sides at all is sad in itself).

The Football Supporters Association made commendable efforts to forge good relations, but they were competing with lurid stories conjured up by the tabloids, intent on selling a few more papers and stirring up an even better story. The F.S.A. produced their own 'English Ambassador' T-shirt and set up an advice centre in Cagliari to help with any problems the fans may have had.

It should be pointed out that, behind the scenes of Italia '90, there was a certain amount of annoyance at the disruption to the lives of ordinary Italians. In addition, there had been bickering over the finances of the tournament. More significantly,two dozen construction workers had been killed in the rush to complete the stadia on time, but the dominant image of football sadly meant that this tragedy was forgotten in the media circus.

The English following was still largely made up of young white men, this could change if the violence associated with England's matches abroad diminishes. The followers of most of the other countries had a higher proportion of women and children. There was no menace hanging over the other partying fans with their faces painted in national colours. All the fans at the World Cup were patriotic, but none were as nationalistic as the English and no others repeatedly sang their national anthems.

The president of UEFA, Georges Johansson, declared that the incident before the England match against Holland made the re-entry of English clubs into Europe unlikely. Again, this is an example of media hype and police over-reaction almost destroying the good work done by the majority of fans.The West Germany match against Yugoslavia had seen extremely violent scenes outside the ground, damage done to shops and 43 Germans were deported - but this was quickly forgotten.

A more blatant example of the discrimination against soccer fans was the incident at the 'Rose and Crown' pub on the evening before the match against Belgium. Italy had just beaten Uruguay and Italian youths goaded English fans in the pub in Rimini. Several English fans threw glasses, which resulted in the Italian police laying into the English. Rather than arresting the troublemakers on both sides, the police rounded up any English fan in the area and duly expelled about 250 from Italy. The press labelled all as the scum of the earth, despite the fact that none were charged or convicted of any offence. Any other troublemaker on holiday might have expected a fine, but not football fans and the vast majority had done nothing at all.

The government and press in England had conjured up such a picture of the fans, that all were treated almost as terrorists. The mayor of Turin urged that the semi-final against West Germany be played elsewhere because of fears of revenge by Juventus fans for the Heysel disaster.

In general, the behaviour of the English fans was remarkably good, considering the provocation they were subjected to by Italian youths, police and the press. The incidents that appeared on our T.V. sets were blown out of all proportion and were usually very minor. The irony is that there was far more trouble in England after the matches against the Cameroons and West Germany. There was little opportunity for the English fans to prove that they were actually only interested in the football, but at least their restraint meant that there were no major incidents ..... and there is only 4 years to U.S.A. '94!

Amazingly, after all the hype surrounding English fans, Colin Moynihan and the government recommended that English clubs be re-admitted to Europe. On a wave of national pride about the success of the England team reaching the semi-finals of the World Cup, it was politically expedient for the government to stage an about turn. On Tuesday 9th July 1990, UEFA gave the announcement that English football fans had been desperate to hear - Manchester United and Aston Villa were to be allowed back into Europe. This was a victory for no-one, but the fans, a realisation that the game of football is more important than the concept of hooliganism, real or imagined. Perhaps this may be the start of a re-appraisal of football fans in general - let's hope so.

WORKING PRESS
85, St. Agnes Place,
Kennington,
London,
SE11 4BB

Other titles published by Working Press:

Working Press books distributed in the U.K. by CENTRAL BOOKS
14, The Leathermarket
London SE1 3ER

Worldwide distribution by COUNTER PRODUCTIONS
P.O. Box 556
London SE5 0RL